revision guides

KT-195-691

DoBrilliantly

ASSociology

Exam practice at its **best**

- **Rob Webb**
- **Series Editor: Jayne de Courcy**

Contents

061196

THE HENLEY COLLEGE LIBRARY

Published by HarperCollins*Publishers* Limited
77–85 Fulham Palace Road
London W6 8JB

www.**Collins**Education.com
On-line support for schools and colleges

© HarperCollins*Publishers* Ltd 2001

First published 2001
10 9 8 7 6 5 4 3
ISBN 0 00 710704 8

Rob Webb asserts the moral right to be identified as the author of this work.

All rights reserved. No part of this publication may be reproduced, stored in a retrieval system, or transmitted in any form or by any means, electronic, mechanical, photocopying, recording or otherwise, without either the prior permission of the Publisher or a licence permitting restricted copying in the United Kingdom issued by the Copyright Licensing Agency Ltd, 90 Tottenham Court Road, London W1P 0LP. This book is sold subject to the condition that it shall not by way of trade or otherwise be lent, hired out or otherwise circulated without the Publisher's prior consent.

British Library Cataloguing in Publication Data
A catalogue record for this book is available from the British Library

Edited by Steve Attmore
Production by Kathryn Botterill
Cover design by Susi Martin-Taylor
Book design by Gecko Limited
Printed and bound in China by Imago

Acknowledgements
The Author and Publishers are grateful to the following for permission to reproduce copyright material:

AQA Specimen examination questions (pp. 14–15, 24–25, 34–35, 44–45, 54–55, 64–65 and 74–75) are reproduced by permission of the Assessment and Qualifications Alliance. The author is responsible for the answers/commentaries on the questions; they have neither been provided nor approved by the AQA and they may not necessarily constitute the only possible solutions.

The extracts from *Inequalities in Health* on page 24 are reproduced by kind permission of Her Majesty's Stationery Office. Permission for the other text extracts are as stated on the page.

Every effort has been made to contact the holders of copyright material, but if any have been inadvertently overlooked, the Publishers will be pleased to make the necessary arrangements at the first opportunity.

Illustrations
Cartoon artwork – Roger Penwill

Photographs
The publishers would like to thank the following for permission to reproduce photographs (T = Top, B = Bottom, L= Left, R = Right):

Steve Attmore, 73 TL;
Photo from www.JohnBirdsall.co.uk, 13;
Format Photographers/Ulrike Preuss 23, Paula Solloway 63, Maggie Murray 73 L and R;
Sally & Richard Greenhill 33, 43.

You might also like to visit:
www.**fire**and**water**.com
The book lover's website

How this book will help you
by Rob Webb

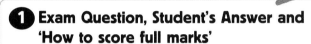

Exam practice — how to answer questions better

This book will help you to improve your performance in your AS Sociology exam.

Every year I mark exam papers where students don't use the information that they've learnt as effectively as they could. This means they don't get the grade they're capable of achieving.

To get a high grade in AS Sociology you need a good grasp of the subject matter **and good exam technique**. Your textbook can help you develop your knowledge and understanding. **This book will help you improve your exam technique, so that you can make the most effective use of what you know**.

Each chapter in this book is broken down into four separate elements, aimed at giving you the guidance and practice you need to improve your exam technique:

❶ Exam Question, Student's Answer and 'How to score full marks'

Each chapter starts with an exam question of the sort you will find on a real AS Sociology paper, followed by a typical student's answer.

The 'How to score full marks' sections show **you where and how the answers could be improved**, e.g. by explaining what the question is asking for, by pointing out missing knowledge etc. **This means that when you meet these sorts of questions in your exam, you will know how to tackle them successfully**.

For parts (e) and (f) of each question – which are worth many more marks – I have also written a paragraph-by-paragraph commentary alongside the student's answer, pointing out what is good, what is not so good and what is missing. **This makes clear what examiners such as myself are looking for in order to award marks**.

❷ 'Don't forget...' boxes

These boxes highlight some of the most common mistakes I see every year in students' **exam papers**. These include both sociological errors (such as writing about the wrong aspect of a topic) and faulty exam technique.

When you're doing your last minute revision, you can quickly read through these boxes.

❸ 'Key points to remember'

The 'Key points to remember' page of each chapter gives you a quick overview of the topic as a whole and lists the most important points that you will need to cover when revising that topic. But remember – a book of this size can't hope to cover all the detailed sociological information you need for your exam – that's what your textbook and class notes are for!

❹ Question to try, Answers and Examiner's hints and comments

Each chapter ends with **an exam question for you to try answering**. Don't cheat! Sit down and try to answer as if you were in an exam. Try to remember all that you've read earlier in the chapter and put it into practice here. To help you, **I've included a couple of 'Examiner's hints' giving you some tips on how to tackle the longer parts of the question**.

When you've written your answer, check it through and then turn to the back of the book. There you'll find an answer to the question you've just done. This answer is of a very good 'A' grade standard. **I've added my 'Examiner's comments' to show you exactly why it's such a good answer**.

Compare your answer with the answer given. If you feel that yours wasn't as good, **you can use the one given and my comments on it to help you decide which aspects of your answer you could improve on**.

The chances are that you are studying the AQA exam board's AS Sociology specification – which is the one that most students sit. The other exam board for AS Sociology is OCR. **The questions in this book are written in the same style as the AQA exam questions, and some of them are actual AQA specimen questions**. However, the OCR questions are very similar in style, so what's in this book **will help you prepare for either AQA or OCR exams**.

I have outlined below some of the **main features of AS Sociology exam questions**. My comments are based on the AQA exam papers. Where OCR papers are different, I have pointed this out.

The main types of questions you will meet

Data-response Items

Sometimes called stimulus-response Items, these are pieces of material for you to use in answering the questions. They may be extracts of text from Sociology books (including textbooks), newspaper and magazine articles, etc. They may be tables of figures, charts, graphs, diagrams or even photographs. Remember that the Items are there to help you. In fact, **many of the questions actually instruct you to use the Items – so unless you want to throw marks away, make sure you do use them**!

Shorter questions

A typical AQA AS exam question is worth 60 marks. It is usually made up of four shorter questions worth 20 marks altogether – a third of the total – plus two longer questions.

The shorter questions often ask you **to explain or define key sociological terms and concepts, to suggest examples or identify and explain reasons, factors, criticisms, etc. connected with the topic**. Many of these shorter questions are linked to the Items – for example, you may be asked to explain the meaning of a term used in an Item – but some of them may simply test the knowledge that you bring to the exam.

Longer questions

The two longer questions are worth 20 marks each – **two-thirds of the total for the whole question**. They are a bit like mini-essays. Some of them will instruct you to use material from an Item in answering the question. One of these two longer questions will normally be an 'assess' question. The other longer question may well ask you to 'explain' or 'examine'. See the section on page 6 on 'command words' for an explanation of these terms.

OCR questions

OCR exam questions are generally quite similar to the AQA questions described above, but you should note the following differences:
● **Two of the three papers are marked out of 90, not 60**. These papers have data-response Items.
● The other paper consists of **a choice of two-part questions on different topics**. The second part of each question is an essay and there are no data-response Items.

The AQA specification for AS Sociology has **seven topics, organised into three modules**. (Most of these topics also appear on the OCR specification for AS or A2 Sociology.) The table below shows how this book covers the topics for both the AQA and the OCR exams.

The topics covered by your specification

AQA topics	Chapter in this book	OCR topics
Families & Households (AS Module 1)	1	Family (AS Module 2)
Health (AS Module 1)	2	Health (A2 Module 5)*
Mass Media (AS Module 1)	3	Mass Media (AS Module 2)
Education (AS Module 2)	4	Education (A2 Module 5)*
Wealth, Poverty & Welfare (AS Module 2)	5	part of Social Policy & Welfare (A2 Module 5)*
Work & Leisure (AS Module 2)	6	part of Social Inequality and Difference (A2 Module 8)*
Sociological Methods (AS Module 3)	7	Sociological Research Skills (AS Module 3)

* Topics with an asterisk are examined by OCR at A2 not at AS level. A2 is the second year of an A level course.

What you have to study

For the AQA AS Sociology exam, you have to sit three papers. **Each paper examines a module of study**. For AQA, these modules are:

1 Families & Households; Health; Mass Media.
2 Education; Wealth, Poverty & Welfare; Work & Leisure.
3 Sociological Methods

You must study at least one topic from each module and answer a question on it in the paper. So, for example, you could study and answer a question on Mass Media in unit 1, on Education in unit 2, and Sociological Methods in unit 3 (where there is just one compulsory topic). However, for unit 3, your school or college may decide to enter you for the Coursework Task instead of the written exam. You should check with your teacher about this.

For OCR AS Sociology, the basics are very similar but the topics are allocated differently to the different modules. These are as follows:

1 The Individual and Society
2 Culture and Socialisation (one topic from Family; Mass Media; Religion; Youth and Culture)
3 Sociological Research Skills (or Research Report)

- **Use the Items**. They're there to help you and, if you don't use them when the question tells you to, you'll be throwing away marks. To make the most of the Items, **read them through several times, picking out or underlining key points and letting your mind digest them**. Think how they link up with your own knowledge.

- **Make a brief plan before writing**. Stick to it and refer back to it throughout when writing your answer.

- **Allocate your time sensibly**. Use the marks available as a rough guide to how much to write.

- **In short questions, if asked for more than one point, start each point on a separate line**. Add extra points if you want – you won't be penalised for wrong ones, but you'll be rewarded for right ones.

- **Know the meaning of the key command words**:
  - **'Explain what is meant by...'** In a short question, this means define the term or concept given, using different words from those in the question. An example alone, while it will throw some light on the point, will not be enough on its own to answer such a question fully. Watch out also for terms that might have a slightly different meaning from their everyday meaning when used by sociologists.
  - **'Identify...'** Here you must show that you can recognise an argument, example, idea, fact, viewpoint, etc. (depending on what the question is about) and briefly explain/describe it. You need to develop further the point you have identified to show your understanding of it.
  - **'Explain...'** In an essay or mini-essay, you must show a detailed knowledge and understanding of something, and apply it in a relevant way to the question. This often implies you need to know **'why'** as well.
  - **'Examine...'** You must consider in detail the relevant information (arguments, evidence, concepts, views, etc.).
  - **'Using material from Item B...'** You must select relevant information from the Item and use it to help answer the question. Remember – there may be more than one point you could use from the Item.
  - **'Assess...'** Here you must show the skill of **evaluation**, weighing up arguments and/or evidence for and against, considering different viewpoints, and drawing an appropriate conclusion. Sometimes you may be asked to assess the strengths and limitations, or the advantages and disadvantages. Look at both sides and draw a conclusion as to whether one side outweighs the other, based on your arguments and evidence for each.

Exam Question and Answer

Item A

Functionalist sociologists have argued that with the transition from pre-industrial society to industrial society, the family has undergone a change in its structure. For example, Talcott Parsons has argued that while in pre-industrial society the family is extended in structure, in industrial society the nuclear family becomes the dominant family structure. 5

Some sociologists also argue that the modern family is much more equal than in the past. For example, Willmott and Young claim that in today's 'symmetrical' nuclear family, husbands' and wives' conjugal roles have become much more similar than in the patriarchal family of the Victorian era. However, feminists have criticised this view of the modern family. Sociologists and historians have also argued that the position of 10 children in the family and in society has changed greatly since pre-industrial times.

Item B

The last three decades of the twentieth century showed two very striking trends:

1. a decline in the number of first marriages, that is, marriages where neither partner had been married previously;

2. a rise in the number of divorces.

Compared with the figures for the early 1970s, the statistics for the late 1990s showed 5 about half as many marriages and twice as many divorces. Although Great Britain had the highest divorce rate in Europe, the same trends were evident elsewhere, especially in the more economically developed and less religious countries of northern Europe.

There has also been a slow decline in the number of religious marriage ceremonies and a corresponding rise in the number of civil marriages in registry offices. However, 10 while most first marriages take place in church, among those couples where one or both partners had already been married before, only about one in five of marriage ceremonies took place in church.

THE HENLEY COLLEGE LIBRARY

SARAH'S ANSWER

(a) What is meant by the patriarchal family (**Item A, line 9**)? [2 marks]

> A family found in a society which is patriarchal.

0/2

(b) Suggest **three** reasons why children's position in the family has changed. [6 marks]

> 1. Because they now have to go to school (compulsory).
> 2. Because the birth rate has fallen, i.e. fewer per family.
> 3. Because of changes in wider society.

4/6

(c) Suggest **two** criticisms which feminist sociologists might make of the view that husbands and wives are now equal. [4 marks]

> 1. There is still domestic violence by men towards women.
> 2. Men and women have different functions.

2/4

(d) Identify and briefly describe **two** factors which may have produced greater equality between the roles of husbands and wives. [8 marks]

> 1. Women now go out to work more than in the past. This means that they can have more financial say in the family, e.g. in decisions about what to spend money on, since now they are contributing financially — i.e. they are now breadwinners as well as homemakers.
> 2. Availability of female contraception has also led to greater equality between the sexes.

6/8

How to score full marks

(a) Sarah merely recycles the question. You need to **define patriarchal using different words**, e.g. as meaning a male-dominated family.

(b) Sarah's first two reasons, though a bit brief, are relevant and correct, but her **third reason is very vague** – what changes? A third reason you could give is the introduction of **laws forbidding child labour** (which has meant that children have become more of an expense for parents, rather than an asset producing an income from an early age).

(c) Sarah's second point scores no marks because **the meaning is unclear and not linked particularly to feminism**. (It needs to be spelt out more fully and clearly.) A better point you could make is to say that although married women are much more likely to go out to work nowadays, **they are still expected to do most of the housework and childcare**.

(d) Sarah only scores 2 marks out of a possible 4 for the second factor because although she makes a good point, **she doesn't describe or explain it properly**. It would have been better to say that availability of female contraception (such as the pill) has **taken away men's power** to decide how many children their wives will bear, when they will have them, etc.

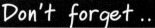

Don't forget ...

When asked to define a term, use **different** words from those in the question itself.

Make sure you spell out your explanations **clearly**!

8

(e) Outline the arguments and evidence for and against the functionalist view of the relationship between industrialisation and family structures (**Item A**).   [20 marks]

SARAH'S ANSWER

To answer this, we must first define 'a family', including a nuclear and extended family. A family is a group of people characterised by shared residence, economic cooperation and related by marriage/blood. A nuclear family is married parents plus children, whereas an extended family involves three or more generations.

According to Murdock, the family performs four functions: sex, reproduction, education (socialisation), and economic. For example, unless the next generation are properly socialised, society would die out. As a result, the family exists everywhere — it is universal. Even though other institutions could perform the functions (e.g. the Israeli kibbutz), the family is the most practical way of doing so.

According to Parsons, there is a fit between the type of society and type of family structure. As Item A says, 'Parsons has argued that while in pre-industrial society the family is extended in structure, in industrial society the nuclear family becomes the dominant family structure'. An example of this is in pre-industrial agricultural societies like Ireland, where one study found that families lived in extended units, sharing agricultural production and consumption. These were male-headed and the eldest son inherited the family farm from his father. This was known as the classic extended family.

In modern society, though, the nuclear family is dominant, because it fits the needs of industry. Modern industry needs a mobile workforce that can move to where the jobs are (unlike farming). If workers lived in big extended families, they wouldn't be mobile enough and the economy would suffer. Also, having nuclear families cuts down the conflict between generations. For example, if the father was a road sweeper but his son became a doctor, the son would 'outrank' his own father. This can't happen in pre-industrial society as the son depends on his father's good will.

9/20

Sarah hasn't made her sociological knowledge relevant to the set question.

Still no mention of industrialisation! She's not linking her knowledge to the question.

At last – the key point that functionalists see a 'fit' between type of society and family structure. Relevant use of the Item, and useful evidence from a study. Explain why the extended family fits pre-industrial society.

Good points about the nuclear family fitting the needs of industrial society, but then she just stops! Write a brief conclusion.

9

How to score full marks

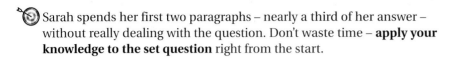

Sarah spends her first two paragraphs – nearly a third of her answer – without really dealing with the question. Don't waste time – **apply your knowledge to the set question** right from the start.

The question asks you to 'outline the arguments and evidence for and against' (i.e. show your evaluation skills), but Sarah hasn't done the 'against' side at all! So, **an absolute 'must' is something against the functionalist view**.

For example, **you could use the historical studies by Laslett, Anderson or Willmott and Young** to criticise the view that the pre-industrial household was extended (Laslett), or that early industrialisation brought about nuclear family structures – both Anderson and Willmott and Young argue that it brought about working-class extended families.

You can also point out that in any given 'type' of society (industrial, pre-industrial, etc.) there may in fact be **several** types of family structure, not just one (as functionalists assume). **Recent trends to greater family diversity** (including lone-parent, reconstituted, gay, one-person households, etc.) may support this view.

Sarah's answer ends abruptly, without a conclusion. Make sure you write **a brief conclusion pulling your main 'for and against' points together**.

Don't forget ...

Keep focused on the question. Make sure that your material is **relevant**, and that you show the examiner **why** it is. Make a plan. Ask yourself: how am I going to make each piece of information relevant to this question?

Read the question – and do what it asks! If it says 'for and against', make sure you do both.

(f) Using material from **Item B** and elsewhere, assess sociological explanations of changes in the rates of marriage and divorce.

[20 marks]

SARAH'S ANSWER

According to the Item, marriage rates have generally decreased and divorce has increased in the UK. Industrialisation has seen a turn around in the way the family functions, and it is possible to analyse the rates within a sociological context.

Good start – uses the Item, and hints that sociologists can tell us something about it.

The divorce rate has increased due to a wide range of factors. Women are no longer the property of men. The Divorce Act has meant that women can now divorce men, and that factors other than infidelity can be used for reasons to divorce. This has seen a dramatic increase in family breakdown, but a subsequent reduction in marital violence. Dennis says that when the sexual attraction and love go between a couple, there is no need to stay married. People stay together far less for the sake of dependent children now. The stigma attached to divorce is not such an issue.

She identifies some explanations for increases in divorce rate – but she needs to *assess* them.

Marriage rates have also fallen for several reasons. Women are under less pressure now to marry and it is quite common to see unmarried women in their thirties. Women are more independent and can manage without a husband financially. They see that a family does not have to be the sole purpose in life, and so many now remain single. Radical feminists believe love is a myth made up by capitalist society to encourage women to marry. This view seems a little harsh, but it is nevertheless a reason for women not to marry. Many women now put their career first and will stay single or cohabit.

Some explanations of marriage rates – but only a hint of assessment (of radical feminism). Explain *why* women are now more independent.

Dennis believes the decrease in marriage is due to a loss of family functions – bureaucratic agencies are taking them over. It seems the modernisation of society and the family has resulted in this decline of marriage and increase in divorce. In a society where the family's functions are more or less catered for by the state apparatuses, the need to marry is less important.

Useful to link falling marriage rates to wider social changes.

The Rapoports see the single-parent family as an important emerging family type. Reconstituted families are increasingly popular. Many people remarry now, and these families contribute to family diversity in the UK.

The point about 'emerging family type' isn't linked to the question. Maybe not the best point on which to end – answer needs 'tying up' more.

12/20

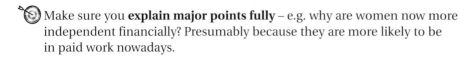

How to score full marks

🎯 Make sure you **explain major points fully** – e.g. why are women now more independent financially? Presumably because they are more likely to be in paid work nowadays.

🎯 Make sure you **link all your points to the question clearly**. For example, what is the relevance of the point about the single-parent family being an 'emerging family type'?

🎯 **Make good use of the Item**. Sarah makes some use of it, but you could do more. For example, it refers to **trends in civil and religious marriage ceremonies** – so you could suggest some reasons for these patterns. For example, secularisation – the decline of religion in modern society – could be a cause of the decline in religious ceremonies, or perhaps as more divorcees try to remarry, they are barred by the clergy from doing so in church.

🎯 The question asks you to '**assess** sociological explanations'. This means that you must look at **the strengths and weaknesses of different explanations**:

  – in terms of evidence for or against them;
  – or by criticising them from the viewpoint of other explanations or perspectives.

For example, you could contrast feminist with functionalist or New Right views of why the divorce rate has risen. 'Sociological explanations' often means 'different perspectives'.

🎯 Remember, as Sarah does, to **deal with both parts of the question** – i.e. both marriage and divorce – even if you find yourself saying more about one than the other.

🎯 **Put Sarah's last paragraph earlier** – as it stands, **the answer ends abruptly** and is not well focused on the question.

🎯 **Write a conclusion** summing up the main explanations and saying something about their usefulness. You could develop Sarah's penultimate paragraph further as a conclusion by arguing that the loss of functions, growing individualism, and greater independence for women, have all led to what Giddens calls a pattern of 'coupling and uncoupling' rather than 'marriage and the family'.

Don't forget ...

Use the Item – especially when the question tells you to! It's there to help you, so study it carefully.

If you're asked to 'assess', do so. Give **strengths** and **weaknesses**, arguments or evidence **for** and **against** the views or explanations you're asked to assess.

Key points to remember

Perspectives on the family: Functionalists stress the positive functions the family performs for society and its members. The **New Right**, like functionalists, see the heterosexual nuclear family as essential to social stability. By contrast, **feminists** and **Marxists** see it as an oppressive, exploitative institution benefiting only men (patriarchy) or capitalism.

The family and social change – history of the family: Functionalists argue that there is a 'fit' between pre-industrial society and the extended family, and industrial society and the nuclear family. But some historical evidence suggests that nuclear families may have been widespread *before* industrialisation, and that industrialisation itself produced extended working-class families. Others argue that family structure has gone through several stages, not just two.

Childhood: Childhood is not a fixed 'thing' – it is **socially constructed** and so varies between times, places and groups. Some argue that it is of recent origin, linked to factors such as industrialisation. Some see it being redefined today, with the impact of the media eroding the boundaries between childhood and adulthood.

The family and social change – family diversity today: Rising rates for divorce, births outside marriage and cohabitation, falling marriage rates, more reconstituted ('step-') families, longer life spans, ethnic diversity, greater toleration of homosexuality, changes in women's position, greater individualism and consumerism, the decline of religion, changes in the law and other trends, are all contributing to greater family diversity. Many writers, including **postmodernists**, argue that this diversity means we can no longer talk about 'the family'. Others disagree, arguing that most of us still live in conventional nuclear families.

State policies and the family: The family doesn't exist in a vacuum but is influenced by other institutions, including the state (or government), whose policies may work to support or undermine different kinds of family. **Feminists** argue that state policy tends to prop up and legitimise (justify) the heterosexual, patriarchal nuclear family and make other family types seem less valid.

Question to try

Item A

The family does not exist in isolation from the rest of society. It is both influenced by what goes on around it, and it acts as an influence on other areas of social life. Wider society, in the form of the mass media, government economic or social policies and the economy, for example, all influence the structure of the family and the roles and relationships of its members. As a result, therefore, sociologists are interested in 5
exploring the interrelationships between the family and the wider social structure. Marxists, for instance, try to identify the different ways in which family life is shaped by the needs of capitalism.

The idea that the family, and the roles and statuses of its members, are shaped by wider society, helps to explain why these can take different forms at different times and 10
places. For example, both the housewife role and the social status that we call 'childhood' today are not the same everywhere and at all times in history. Rather than being 'natural' or biologically determined, they are both in fact socially constructed.

Item B

Ann Oakley has described the image of the typical or 'conventional' family as 'nuclear families composed of legally married couples, voluntarily choosing the parenthood of one or more (but not too many) children'. Leach has called this the 'cereal packet image of the family'. The image of the happily married couple with two children is prominent in advertising and the 'family sized' packets of cereals and other products 5
are aimed at just this type of grouping.

However, the view that this image equals reality has been attacked. Robert and Rhona Rapoport draw attention to the fact that in 1978, for example, just 20% of families consisted of couples with children in which there was a single breadwinner. There has been a steady decline in the proportion of households consisting of married couples 10
with dependent children, from 38% of all households in 1961 to 28% in 1987.

The Rapoports argue that this change is part of the growing diversity of family forms in Britain today. They identify five types of diversity:

1. organisational
2. cultural
3. class
4. life cycle
5. generational.

Source: adapted from M. Haralambos and M. Holborn,
Sociology: Themes and Perspectives, 5th edition (Collins Educational, 2000).

(a) According to **Item B**, by how many percentage points did the proportion of households consisting of married couples with dependent children fall between 1961 and 1987?

[2 marks]

(b) Suggest **two** other features of the typical 'cereal packet family' apart from those described by Oakley (**Item B**, **lines 1–3**).

[4 marks]

(c) Suggest **three** government economic or social policies which might influence the structure of the family or the roles and relationships of its members (**Item A**, **lines 3–5**).

[6 marks]

(d) Identify and briefly describe **two** ways in which the family might be 'shaped by the needs of capitalism' (**Item A**, **lines 7–8**).

[8 marks]

(e) Examine the arguments and evidence for the view that both childhood and the housewife role are socially constructed (**Item A**, **lines 11–13**).

[20 marks]

(f) Using material from **Item B** and elsewhere, assess sociological contributions to an understanding of the diversity of family forms found in society today.

[20 marks]

Examiner's hints

- In part (e), remember to deal with both. Explain what 'social construction' means and link the rise of childhood and the housewife role to social changes like industrialisation, compulsory schooling, etc.
- In part (f), you must **evaluate** different sociological views, not just describe them. Look at different perspectives – e.g. functionalist, New Right, feminist, postmodernist. And remember to use the Item – e.g. the Rapoports' five types.

Answers can be found on pages 76–78.

Item A

Of the population of England and Wales, those people born in the Indian sub-continent have higher than average rates of tuberculosis, heart disease and diabetes, but lower rates of certain cancers. Those born in Africa or the Caribbean have higher rates of strokes, diabetes and high blood pressure. About a third of all male deaths in the UK are from circulatory diseases (such as heart attacks and strokes), but this rises to about   5 a half among men under 50 from the Indian sub-continent, while Indian men in their 20s have over three times the national death rate from heart disease. Those born in Africa, the Caribbean and the Indian sub-continent are also more likely to suffer death from accidents.

There are also important differences in the birth weight of babies born to different   10 ethnic groups. The average birth weight of babies born to mothers from India, Bangladesh and East Africa is about 300 grams lower than for babies of women who were born in the UK. These differences in some ways mirror social class differences; for example, babies born to working-class mothers have a lower average birth weight than those born to middle-class mothers.   15

Item B

It is well known that there is a class gradient in health. Yet in working-class areas, the provision of healthcare resources, such as GPs, opticians, dental surgeons, clinics and hospitals, tends to be less than the provision in middle-class areas.

These geographical and class-related inequalities in health care are found both nationally and locally. Different health authorities spend widely varying amounts of   5 money and may have different priorities. For example, a given kind of health care – such as infertility treatment, for instance – which is available in one area may not be available in a neighbouring area, or only be available to more restricted groups of patients.

TARIQ'S ANSWER

(a) What is meant by 'a class gradient in health' (**Item B, line 1**). [2 marks]

A gradient is a slope.

 0/2

(b) Suggest **two** reasons why babies born to working-class mothers weigh less on average than babies born to middle-class mothers (**Item A, lines 14–15**). [4 marks]

One reason is because working-class mothers are less likely to know about nutrition during pregnancy.

Another is that middle-class women are more likely to breastfeed, so their babies thrive.

 2/4

(c) Suggest **three** reasons why women on average live longer than men in modern society. [6 marks]

Women live longer than men because they don't smoke as much as men, so don't get lung cancer etc. as much.

Secondly, they go to the doctor's more than men (e.g. to take the kids), so are more likely to get early medical attention which can sometimes save their lives.

A third reason is that they are biologically different from men and this accounts for the longer life expectancy.

 4/6

(d) Identify and briefly describe **two** ways in which sociologists can contribute to our understanding of disability. [8 marks]

One way is by showing how social factors can cause disability. For example, manual workers are more likely to have accidents at work than professional workers.

Another way sociologists can help us understand disability is by seeing it as a label.

 6/8

How to score full marks

(a) A gradient *is* a slope, but this doesn't really answer the question. A class gradient in health is the idea that as one moves **down the social class scale, health also declines**.

(b) Tariq's first reason is a good one but his second one isn't – as a mother can't breastfeed until after the baby is born, this can't increase birth weight! Better reasons would be that working-class mothers are more likely to have **premature** babies, more likely to miss **ante-natal appointments** and more likely to **smoke** and to **drink alcohol** during pregnancy.

(c) His first two reasons are fine, but the third one isn't. If he had been able to say **which** biological differences were important or **how** they prolonged women's lives, he might have had a chance, but as it stands it's not very convincing. It would have been better to suggest some other aspects of **lifestyle or social role**, such as that **women don't drive or drink as much as men** (both dangerous activities, especially if combined!) – or don't work in more **dangerous jobs** like mining, construction or deep-sea fishing as much as men.

(d) One way to tackle this question, which Tariq has done to some extent, is to think of **disability as both socially caused and socially constructed**. Disability can be **caused** by social factors like work, and Tariq has identified and described this. Disability can also be seen as socially **constructed** – in other words, it's a label or definition applied to some people by others. Tariq sees this, too, but for full marks he needs to go on to **describe** it. He could have said that once labelled as disabled, a person may be **treated differently** (e.g. patronised, ignored, seen as not fully human, etc.).

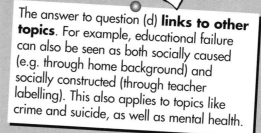

Don't forget ...

When asked to 'identify and briefly describe', **make sure you go on to spell out the description by giving an example or some further development of the point you have identified**. That way, you'll pick up the other half of the available marks.

The answer to question (d) **links to other topics**. For example, educational failure can also be seen as both socially caused (e.g. through home background) and socially constructed (through teacher labelling). This also applies to topics like crime and suicide, as well as mental health.

(e) Examine sociological explanations of differences in the health chances of different ethnic groups, such as those shown in **Item A**.

[20 marks]

TARIQ'S ANSWER

As Item A shows, different ethnic groups have different health chances, and ethnic minorities tend to have worse health than the white majority in Britain. There are various reasons for this difference which sociologists have tried to identify.

One factor is genetic. For example, black people are more likely to get inherited diseases like sickle cell anaemia, which is very rare in white people.

Other causes can be to do with culture. For example if a group has a particular norm which requires women to marry very young and not go out to work but to stay at home, and the religion of the group forbids them to use contraception, then it is likely that there will be a high birth rate and the risk of worse health for both mother and children. Some groups also practise female circumcision which can be harmful.

Another example of how a group's culture can affect the health of ethnic minorities is in the fact that Asian children have higher rates of rickets (a bone deformity) as a result of their diet, which lacks vitamin D. Some sociologists have also argued that this is also due to wearing clothes which cover up so much of the skin and prevent sunlight reaching it (sunlight helps to produce vitamin D).

Another factor is language. If a person's first language is not English, they may not be able to communicate with doctors, nurses etc., so they may fail to get the treatment they need. It might also mean that they won't be able to understand health education campaigns and advice, so this will also worsen their health chances.

Housing can also be a cause of ill health. Ethnic minority groups can find that their housing is substandard. Marxists or conflict theorists would argue that this is the result of discrimination against minorities, so that they get pushed into the worst housing, with overcrowding, damp etc., and this in turn leads to health problems for the family members.

Although minorities have worse health than the majority of the population, it can be difficult to explain partly because we don't have proper figures, e.g. in Item A it only tells us about people who were born in India, Africa and the Caribbean, but a lot of the minorities were born in the UK so they wouldn't appear in the figures.

11/20

Tariq makes brief use of the Item to set up the question. He now needs to outline more patterns, or to look at sociological explanations.

Not really a sociological explanation. He needs to link it to the question.

This is better, with good points about how culture can affect health, but it's a bit hypothetical – *which* ethnic group(s) does this refer to?

Relevant material, but a bit one-sided. Tariq could look at cultural practices of minorities which promote good as well as bad health.

Good points. It's worth linking this paragraph to the previous ones about cultural factors.

Useful points. As these are structural issues it would be worth saying so, and more theory would be welcome.

Interesting and relevant point about the statistics. He could also ask why figures aren't collected on UK-born minorities. Needs a conclusion.

How to score full marks

A good way to approach this question would be to **identify different types of explanation**. These could be, for instance, **cultural**, **structural and biological**. You can then organise your answer into sections on each, with an account of the explanation followed by some evidence for (or against) it.

Tariq gives a **genetic** or biological explanation. There is nothing wrong with bringing non-sociological explanations into answers, but you must **use them to help answer the question**. For example, Tariq could have used it after looking at sociological explanations, as a **way of evaluating** them.

Tariq makes brief **reference to the Item**, but there's a lot more in there you could use. You could link **low birthweight** to poverty among minorities (who are more likely to be working class), and ask why minorities are at greater risk of **accidental death** (e.g. link to working conditions, housing, etc.). Does **racism and discrimination** cause stress and affect high blood pressure and strokes?

Look at **mental as well as physical health**. Some studies indicate that black people are more likely to be labelled schizophrenic, given harsher treatment and be 'sectioned' against their will. Is this because of institutional racism, more stressful lives, or both?

Try to **apply some theory**. Tariq mentions **Marxism/conflict theory**. You could develop this. You could also look at **functionalism**, via the idea that minorities do not fully share the mainstream 'modern' culture and therefore may be engaging in unenlightened practices harmful to health. You could criticise this theory as **ethnocentric**, though.

Don't forget ...

You should try to **identify** and **discuss** types of explanations, not just list various factors.

Make use of the Item wherever you can – it's there to give you clues and cues as to what to write.

(f) Using material from **Item B** and elsewhere, assess sociological explanations of geographical and class inequalities in health care.

[20 marks]

TARIQ'S ANSWER

It iis well known that the working class have worse health than the middle class in Britain. This is because they lead less healthy lives, e.g. more smokers and heavy drinkers are working class and they don't take as much exercise or take care of their diet as much as middle-class people do. Also their worse health is because of their jobs which are more likely to be dangerous, e.g. on a building site or polluted factory, and their income is lower so they can't afford a healthy lifestyle anyway.

> Tariq tells us about class inequalities in health chances, rather than in health care. He needs to link these together.

Another problem they (the working class) face is that in their areas there aren't as many facilities, such as GPs and hospitals, clinics, etc, so this means waiting lists are longer and they don't get the treatment they need when they need it.

> This is better, but brief. He needs to say why facilities are worse in working-class areas.

Another group of people whose health care is underfunded is the elderly. This is partly because old age can't be 'cured' so it isn't a very glamorous area for doctors to work in and also the old have quite a low status in modern society so it is not surprising that funds for their health care are also low.

> This isn't made relevant to the question, as it's not about either class or geographical inequalities.

As Item B says, there are also regional or geographical inequalities in health care, with some areas spending more than others. This is sometimes called 'postcode prescribing', where for example a treatment or drug is available in one area but not in another. The government have recently been trying to do something about this to even things out, but it still remains. Often the middle-class areas get the highest funding for NHS care, even though they don't need it as much. This might fit with Marxist theory that capitalist society works to benefit the higher classes, and this seems to go for health care.

> Useful points about postcode prescribing, higher funding for middle-class areas, and a bit of theory. He needs to develop the theory further – e.g. say why capitalist society works like this, and how this links to health spending.

Middle-class people can always queue jump by going private if they need an operation or other treatment urgently, which is not something that most working-class patients could afford to do. Also they are more likely to know how to get what they require from the NHS than the working class, e.g. Howlett and Ashley found when they studied middle-class and working-class men with the same disease that the middle-class men got higher quality treatment, top doctors and hospitals etc. and were treated before their condition got worse, whereas working-class males had to wait longer, went to ordinary general hospitals etc., and were less likely to survive or make full recoveries.

> Good point about going private and good example of a study. Could look at other studies of how the middle class get more from the NHS.

11/20

How to score full marks

⊙ This question is about inequalities in health **care**. Don't be tempted to write all you know about inequalities in health **chances** – i.e. which class lives longest or gets sick most often. Obviously, the two are connected – good care can prolong your life or make you well – but health care is only one factor in health chances (diet, exercise, leisure, housing, income etc. are also important).

⊙ A good concept linking unequal health and unequal care is Tudor Hart's '**inverse care law**' which states that that 'the availability of good medical care tends to vary inversely with the need of the population served' – i.e. **those who need most care** (usually the working class) get least.

⊙ The question is also about some **specific** inequalities in care – class and geographical ones. **Keep focused** and don't drift, as Tariq did, into age inequalities – or gender or ethnic inequalities for that matter. Tariq could say a bit more about **geographical** inequalities, e.g. how far are they really class inequalities; how far are they the result of past decisions (e.g. to site a hospital in a particular place)?

⊙ Tariq describes one study at the end, but there are others. Cartwright and O'Brien found that middle-class patients get **longer consultations** with their GP, GPs know them better, etc. Middle-class patients have the **cultural capital** (Bourdieu) or **elaborated speech code** (Bernstein) to communicate effectively with middle-class doctors. You could also look at **material obstacles** in the way of working-class patients – e.g. less able to get paid time off work to attend appointments.

⊙ Look also at **types of care** – the working class make more use of the NHS than the middle class, but less so in relation to their need, and less in terms of **preventative** (vaccinations, check-ups, etc.) and screening services than the middle class. **Quality** of care is harder to measure, but the middle class are more likely to get second opinions, beds in higher status teaching hospitals etc.

⊙ You could also look at different **types of industry** and how they affect health, as well as the **regional factor** (e.g. does living near a power station affect health patterns?).

Don't forget ...

Make sure you say something about **all** major parts of a question – in this case, both class and geographical inequalities – even if you don't write an equal amount about both.

Don't confuse health **chances** and health **care**. They are related, but different, ideas.

Key points to remember

Health, illness and disability: These are not merely biological states or conditions, as the bio-medical model of health suggests. They are also **socially constructed**. This means that what counts as healthy, ill or disabled is not fixed, but varies from one group, place or time to another. For example, studies show that working-class women are less likely to report back pain to their GP because they regard it as 'normal' or 'not an illness'. Similarly, others may label us as disabled, sick or mad and treat us accordingly, and this in turn may affect how we see ourselves. Society also constructs or creates disability in another way – for example, by making buildings inaccessible to those in wheelchairs. The **way society is organised** makes us able or unable to do certain things.

The unequal distribution of health and illness: A basic question for sociologists is, why do members of some social groups have worse health than others? Much of the attention has been on class inequalities in health, where the two main explanations are the **cultural or behavioural approach** and the materialist or structural approach. The first sees health inequalities as the result of differences in behaviour (e.g. working-class people are more likely to smoke) and this in turn is seen as the result of different cultural norms and values (such as a desire for immediate satisfaction without regard to the future). The **materialist or structural approach**, by contrast, emphasises the effect of material factors such as work, unemployment, income and housing upon health. It sees class differences in health-related behaviour (such as smoking) as a response to the pressures caused by the individual's position in the class structure.

Inequalities in provision of and access to care: As well as inequalities in health chances, there are also inequalities in health care. The **'inverse care law'** says that 'the availability of good medical care tends to vary inversely with the need of the population served' – so working-class areas with poorer health are less well provided with health services than middle-class areas with good health. Middle-class patients are also more likely to be articulate, knowledgeable and confident in getting the most from the NHS, and may also have the option of 'going private'. There are also **gender and ethnic differences** in access to care and quality of service obtained, often linked to racism and sexism both in the NHS and in wider society.

Mental illness: This is usually thought of as a subject more for psychologists than sociologists. However, sociology can contribute to our understanding of this issue. Sociologists have taken two kinds of approach to mental health and illness. One approach looks at the **social factors** that affect our mental health, such as housing, work, family life and so on. For example, a lone parent on a low income and living in a tower block is at considerable risk of depression. A second approach is to see mental illness as **socially constructed** – a label applied by some people to others. This approach focuses on why members of some groups are more likely to be labelled as mentally ill, and on what happens to them as a result.

The role of medicine and the health professions: One popular view sees medicine and the health professions, especially doctors, as responsible for our health and for the improvements in life expectancy in modern times. However, many sociologists argue that factors such as better living standards are more important than medical advances. Some sociologists have studied the role of doctors. **Functionalists** argue, for example, that doctors police the sick role to ensure that individuals do not illegitimately evade their role responsibilities by pretending to be sick. Many **Marxists** see the medical profession as benefiting capitalism by keeping the workforce healthy, while **feminists** see doctors as an important part of patriarchal power, exerting control over women's lives, for example in the area of reproduction. **Illich** argues that medicine and the medical profession now enjoy the power and status once afforded to the church, and that whole areas of life have become medicalised.

Item A

One way of studying mental illness is to see it as a type of labelling. This is strikingly illustrated by Rosenhan's (1973) pseudo-patient study, entitled 'On being sane in insane places'. A team of researchers presented themselves at a number of Californian hospitals claiming, falsely, to have been hearing voices. Once admitted, they behaved normally. Yet, having been diagnosed as schizophrenic, all their subsequent behaviour was interpreted by staff in terms of this label. Interestingly, though, some of the other patients suspected that the pseudo-patients were not genuinely ill.

5

Item B

Cultural or behavioural explanations of the distribution of health in modern industrial society give an independent causal role to ideas and behaviour in the onset of disease and the event of death. Such explanations often focus on the individual, emphasising unthinking, reckless or irresponsible behaviour or incautious life-style as the determinant of poor health status. What is implied is that people harm themselves or their children by the excessive consumption of refined foods, lack of exercise and so on.

5

There are class differences in these patterns of behaviour. For example, the bottom income group eats more white bread and sugar, but less brown or wholemeal bread and fresh fruit, than other income groups.

10

Some sociologists see such differences in behaviour as the cause of class inequalities in health and illness. They also argue that these behavioural differences between members of different social classes are the result of sub-cultural differences.

Source: adapted from P. Townsend and N. Davidson (eds), *Inequalities in Health* (Penguin, 1982)

(a) Explain what sociologists mean by the term 'label' (**Item A, line 7**). [2 marks]

(b) Identify **two** differences between working-class and middle-class life-styles which may affect health chances, other than those mentioned in **Item B**. [4 marks]

(c) Suggest **three** ways in which the label 'schizophrenic' may adversely affect the person labelled. [6 marks]

(d) Identify and briefly describe **two** criticisms of the view that mental illness is the product of labelling by psychiatrists. [8 marks]

(e) Explain why some sociologists argue that medicine and the medical profession have made little or no contribution to improvements in the general health of the population in industrial society. [20 marks]

(f) Using material from **Item B** and elsewhere, assess the view that class inequalities in health and illness are the result of cultural and behavioural differences. [20 marks]

Examiner's hints
- For (e) you need to be aware of some of the reasons for improvements in health in industrial society. These tend to centre on the importance of social and economic factors rather than medical ones.
- For (f), you are being asked to assess – in other words, this question tests the skill of evaluation – so it won't be enough just to *describe* the cultural or behavioural explanation of health inequalities. A good way to evaluate the cultural/ behavioural view is to contrast it with the materialist or structural approach. You should also use evidence from Item B (the question requires that you do this) and from studies you are familiar with on the causes of health inequalities.

Answers can be found on pages 79–81.

Exam Question and Answer

Item A

Women's roles in TV ads 'sexist'

The portrayal of women in television commercials shows the 'very unacceptable face of sexism', according to a study into sexual stereotyping in advertising.

Stereotyping is robust, 'lending strong support to the concern that women exist in what is essentially a man's world', says Dr Guy Cumberbatch, who carried out the study for the Broadcasting Standards Council. Women in commercials are younger and blonder   5
than men and less likely to be shown in a professional setting, the study showed.

Men outnumber women by almost two to one in advertisements, and the vast majority of adverts – 89 per cent – use a male voice.

Men were more than twice as likely to be shown in work settings, how they performed in these jobs was an integral part of the advertiser's message, but when women   10
appeared in work settings, their relationships were emphasised.

Source: adapted from an article by Georgina Henry, *The Guardian* copyright, 21 November 1990

Item B

It is not just a matter of how information is obtained, but also of how events are explained. The Glasgow University Media Group has demonstrated how the news favours explanations that reflect the views of dominant groups in British society. Their content analysis of strike coverage makes this point particularly well, for it is characteristic of strikes that management and unions provide contrasting explanations   5
of them. The television reporting of strikes did recognise that there were two views, but generally privileged the managerial account. Managerial explanations came up more often, were highlighted in headlines and summaries, and were adopted by the journalists themselves. An illusion of balance was created because both views were represented, but there was no real balance because they were weighted differently.   10

Source: adapted from J. Fulcher and J. Scott, *Sociology* (Oxford University Press, 1999)

CAROLINE'S ANSWER

(a) Explain what is meant by 'stereotype'. [2 marks]

A stereotype is for instance where all women are portrayed as housewives when in fact many women have careers of their own.

 1/2

(b) Suggest **two** reasons why journalists might adopt 'managerial explanations' in their reporting of strikes (**Item B, line 7**). [4 marks]

One reason is that it is likely that journalists and managers are from the same social background.

Secondly, journalists and managers may well have had the same education, e.g. private schooling and Oxbridge, so the journalists have sympathy with the managers' views.

 2/4

(c) Identify **three** ways in which people might be influenced by the output of the mass media. [6 marks]

One way is by what they see on television, e.g. if they see an advert they might go out and buy the product it advertises.

A second way is by what they see in films, e.g. if you witness violence you might copy it (the hypodermic needle effect).

A third way is by what they read in the newspaper.

 4/6

(d) Identify and briefly describe **two** criticisms of the view that the owners of the mass media control the output of the mass media. [8 marks]

One criticism is that although the owners actually own the business, they don't take the everyday decisions about what to publish/broadcast. For example, a media company can be owned by thousands of shareholders (e.g. ordinary members of the public or big pension funds) who know nothing about how to produce a newspaper or TV programme — so they have to leave it to the media professionals (editors and journalists) since they know how and what to produce.

Secondly, what pluralists argue is that the output of the media is what the consumers want.

 6/8

THE HENLEY COLLEGE LIBRARY

How to score full marks

(a) Caroline gives a good **example** of a stereotype, **but the question asks for an explanation**. A better answer would be that a stereotype is a simplified (and usually negative) image or label attached to a group, so that **all members of that group are seen as sharing that characteristic** – e.g. all gays are effeminate, or all women have maternal feelings.

(b) The two reasons that Caroline gives are **too similar** – education is part of social background. Another reason she could have given is that journalists favour managerial explanations because they are **told to by their editors or employers**.

(c) Caroline's first two ways are fine – advertising and copycat violence are both ways in which people might be influenced – but **her third point doesn't really say anything** beyond simply identifying newspapers as a source of influence. Part of the problem is that she has begun each of her three ways with a particular medium (television, film, newspapers), which isn't necessary and perhaps not even helpful. Other ways could include having one's **political views** or voting intentions altered, or **giving to a charity** following a televised appeal, for example.

(d) A very full, well-developed first criticism – that the owners wouldn't know how to control the output – earns Caroline four marks. A useful concept is **operational control**: this describes who is responsible for day-to-day decisions about how to run ('operate') media organisations. Caroline's second criticism, though correct, is undeveloped, so it only gets two marks. A useful concept here is **consumer sovereignty** – the idea that the customer is 'king' or 'queen'. Media organisations are usually in business to sell a product (film, newspaper, etc.), so they must produce 'output' that people will buy. It is no good the owners trying to foist off their own preferences onto the consumers – they will just end up making a loss.

Don't forget ...

When asked to explain a term, don't just give an example. A definition – an alternative way of expressing the same idea, using different terms – is a better way to tackle such questions.

When asked for a number of different reasons, examples, points, etc., make sure that they really are different. Watch out for overlap between them, and if in doubt give more points than you've been asked for. Examiners reward the ones that are right!

(e) Outline the sociological arguments and evidence for the view that the reporting of news by the mass media is selective.

[20 marks]

CAROLINE'S ANSWER

There is a lot of evidence gathered by sociologists for the view that the reporting of news in the media is selective, i.e. biased. This can be seen in Item B where the Glasgow University Media Group (GUMG) showed how in strike reporting the reports favoured the management view of events. For example, management would be interviewed in a quiet office whereas the strikers would be interviewed outdoors in the street. Management were usually described as 'offering' more money, etc., whereas the unions were described as 'demanding' a pay rise or 'threatening' a strike. Also, the background was rarely given, so often it looked as if the workers were just going on strike for the hell of it, making them look irrational or easily manipulated by their leaders.

> **Some good use of evidence here. Caroline builds successfully on the Item by adding her own knowledge.**

Other news is also reported in a selective way. For example, there are thousands of crimes committed every day, but only some of them get into the press or TV news. Usually these are sensationalised and often involve violence, so if you went by what you saw or read in the news, you would think there was a lot of violent crime since this is what the media choose to report.

> **Good illustration – but needs explanation of *why* violence is 'news'.**

Some sociologists argue that this is because of news values. These are what editors and journalists go by to decide what stories to select. For example, stories that only develop slowly don't get into the news, like the causes of a famine – it has to be immediate. Galtung and Ruge identify various news values such as immediacy that affect whether a story makes it to the news or not. Another one is negativity, which means if it's bad news it's more likely to get in – nobody wants to know about disasters that don't happen. Also, disasters far away may not be seen as being as interesting as ones nearer to home.

> **Good use of concept of news values and good examples – both help to explain selectivity.**

There are different theories of news. The Marxist theory says that what appears in the news is to benefit the ruling class, e.g. strikes are reported in such a way that the public won't be sympathetic, and generally newspapers take a conservative line on things which oppose radical changes (e.g. talking about the 'loony left' to make it look as if socialists are all mad). The news is ruling class ideology which helps to perpetuate capitalism by discrediting its opponents.

> **Good to see some theory, but would have been better still after the first paragraph, which it would help to explain.**

However, interactionists say that this doesn't just happen, you have to have journalists, editors, etc., selecting certain stories as newsworthy and to present them in a certain way. Interactionists see these professionals as gatekeepers – they let some stories through but not others. They use their sense of news values to decide which stories pass through. (14/20)

> **Relevant points about interactionism, but should briefly say *why* interactionists take this view. She ends a bit abruptly – it needs a conclusion to pull it all together.**

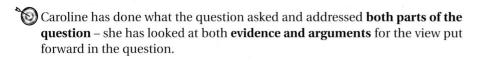 Caroline has done what the question asked and addressed **both parts of the question** – she has looked at both **evidence and arguments** for the view put forward in the question.

However, you could take it further. **Other theories** could be brought in, such as **pluralism** – news reporting is selective because media professionals have to give the consumers what they want (rather than because this is what the ruling class wants, as Marxists argue). **Feminist** views would be worth a mention, or you could look at different **types of Marxism** – **instrumental versus hegemonic**. You could also bring key **interactionist concepts** such as **meaning, social construction or the manufacture of news** into the account of news values, gatekeepers, etc.

Other studies which deal with the reporting of news could be referred to, such as those by **Stuart Hall** on mugging, **Stan Cohen** on mods and rockers, etc.

Other concepts you could draw on include **agenda-setting** and **hierarchies of credibility**. You could think about using **examples** from the coverage of other news topics apart from those that Caroline refers to – e.g. the way **minorities** are marginalised, treatment of the **'royals', soccer hooligans** etc.

Don't forget ...

You should always write a conclusion to pull your answer together and reflect back on the question as a whole. Briefly summarise your points and link them to the set question.

Questions that ask for **'arguments'** need theories and explanations; questions that ask for **'evidence'** need studies and examples (and some of these might be in the Items).

(f) Using material from **Item A** and elsewhere, assess the arguments for the view that the media perpetuate stereotypes of gender.

[20 marks]

CAROLINE'S ANSWER

The media are often accused of portraying women in stereotyped ways as merely housewives, mothers, etc. and also men as always the breadwinners, whereas in fact more and more women are going out to work today though the media often ignore this in their portrayals. Likewise, men may stay at home and be househusbands though this is never portrayed.

Useful to draw attention to stereotypes of men as well as women – but shouldn't exaggerate: are househusbands really *never* portrayed?

The media stereotypes of gender start early on in a child's socialisation. Lobban found in her analysis of children's reading schemes that women and female characters (often these were animals not humans) were generally shown indoors, doing domestic tasks, with the little girls helping their mothers around the house. Boys were shown outdoors more, doing more active things like climbing trees, helping their dads repair the car, etc., and generally showing more initiative than the girls.

Caroline shows good knowledge of a relevant study here (Lobban). It was done in the 1970s, though. Have things changed since?

With these kinds of influences, it's not surprising then that children grow up and perpetuate these things in their own gender roles. There is also the influence of teen magazines which contribute to the socialisation process for girls. One feminist, McRobbie, did a study of 'Jackie' magazine and found it was preoccupied with romance and portrayed teenage girls as aiming to get a boy and keep him as their main aim in life, rather than to be independent.

Relevant, but needs more about McRobbie – and about her more recent work on magazines for young women.

Item A also shows how women are stereotyped into certain roles and assumptions are made about them. Women in adverts are younger and blonder than men, they are less likely to be portrayed in adverts than men and less likely to appear in work settings and if they do, their jobs aren't seen as central, whereas for men their job performance is vital to the message of the ad. This is probably because women aren't 'supposed' to be in paid work according to the stereotype.

Caroline uses the Item, but not very well. She's really just paraphrasing it without adding much apart from her last sentence. Develop it by discussing further *why* women are portrayed this way.

Feminists would say this stereotyping is all because of patriarchy. Radical feminists say society exists for men's benefit, so the media stereotypes women as inferior, over-emotional, etc.

Some theory at last – but not much! Say something about other types of feminism.

By stereotyping women into fixed roles such as housewife, blonde bombshell/sex symbol, etc., the media is restricting them. Meehan ('Ladies of the Evening') studied television programmes in the USA and

> **Some relevant evidence, but needs tying in to the question more.**

found there were only 10 different roles for women, such as the good wife, the witch or the bitch. Tuchman says that the media annihilates women symbolically, i.e. it destroys them/makes them invisible.

> **OK as far as it goes, but brief. Needs to reflect back on the question here.**

All in all, women are portrayed very unfairly by the mass media, being stereotyped into traditional feminine roles. Feminists would argue that this is because society is male-dominated.

11/20

How to score full marks

Caroline makes some reference to both male and female stereotypes, but maybe she could say **more about men** – after all, the question is about gender, not just about women.

Caroline has some useful material from a number of **studies**, although she doesn't always give a very full account of their findings (e.g. more can be said about McRobbie, Tuchman and Meehan).

Likewise, she tells us a little about feminism, but you should **make more use of theory** than Caroline does. The question asks for arguments, and this is what theories will give us. Consider what other **types of feminism** – e.g. liberal and Marxist – would say, as well as other perspectives on the media like **pluralism**.

Caroline's answer is more about presenting information showing that the media stereotypes women than it is about **assessing arguments** for the view that the media **perpetuate** gender stereotypes. You could consider whether the media **create** these stereotypes **or merely reflect** existing ones.

You could also look at **whether things have changed**. Do the media still stereotype women (and men) in the same ways as in Lobban's study? Or have **new stereotypes** emerged (e.g. the sexually liberated young woman portrayed in some magazines, or the 'new man')? If so, why? Is it **because women's – or men's – role has changed**? Similarly, remember there are **different types of media** – do they all portray gender in the same way?

Don't forget ...

> Use the Item, but don't just paraphrase it – **build on it and apply it to the question**.

> With questions on media representations, **don't fall into the trap** of saying the media 'always' portray a group in a certain way – they don't!

Key points to remember

Audiences: Early research focused on the effects of the media on their audiences. The hypodermic syringe or mass manipulative model saw the media as having a **direct, immediate effect** on an audience of passive individuals. Later approaches, such as the two-step flow and uses and gratifications models, argued that the media's effects were more **limited/indirect** and saw the audience as more active, making use of the media to satisfy their needs. **Morley** shows how different groups interpret the same messages differently.

Ideology: Marxists and other sociologists argue that the mass media are a key ideological institution. That is, they produce ideas, beliefs, values, etc. that conceal the reality of exploitation and justify the position of dominant groups in society, such as the ruling class. **Feminists** argue, similarly, that the media's output reinforces male dominance over women. However, **pluralists** argue that many different viewpoints are expressed in the media, not one dominant ideology. **Postmodernists** reject the concept of ideology since they argue that there is no underlying reality being covered up – the media's output *is* reality.

Representations: Evidence for the debate about ideology comes from studies of how different genders, ethnic groups, classes, age groups, disability and sexuality are represented in the media. **Stereotyping** of many such groups is common and **conflict theories** like Marxism and feminism argue that it serves the purpose of subordinating less powerful social groups. However, different media (television, press, film, etc.) and genres (news, drama, sitcoms, etc.) may represent such groups differently, and representations of a group can thus vary, as well as change over time. Some explanations, such as **structuralist Marxism**, focus on the background and values of the professionals who produce media output, while **instrumentalist Marxists** emphasise the interests of media owners and **pluralists** focus on audience preferences.

Selection and presentation of news and other media output: A key idea here is that news is **manufactured**, not discovered. What counts as news is socially constructed – for example, journalists use their sense of what is newsworthy to decide whether and how to report a story. These **news values** include immediacy – stories that take a long time to unfold are less likely to be reported. Journalists and editors are **gatekeepers**, letting some stories through to the audience. A key news value is negativity – bad news is news. **Interactionists** have studied the processes by which news is created; **Marxists** focus on whose interests the news serves. For example, strikes may be reported as bad, strikers as irrational, etc. – all of which serves the interests of their capitalist employers.

Ownership and control: Instrumentalist Marxists argue that media ownership is concentrated in the hands of a few capitalists who use this power to control media output, producing ideology to manipulate the working class into accepting their place. **Structuralist Marxists** do not accept that the owners exert direct control. They argue instead that the media produce a set of ideas or a world-view that reinforces capitalism by making it appear 'natural'. This is produced by media professionals – mainly white, middle-class, middle-aged men who share the general outlook of the capitalist class. **Pluralists** do not regard the issue of ownership and control as particularly important, because for them the consumer is sovereign. The audience decides what the media's output will be, since they are the ones who switch the programmes on or off, or buy or refuse to buy a newspaper. Media owners and professionals must cater to their tastes or lose business.

Question to try

Item A

A content analysis study of actors appearing on British television, conducted in the 1980s for the Commission for Racial Equality, found that in a three-week period, 92.6% of those appearing on BBC1, 96% of those appearing on Granada, and 100% of those appearing on BBC2 were white.

Not only that, but there are important differences in the ways in which white people and members of ethnic minority groups are portrayed by the mass media. For example, black people are often treated in newspapers as a social problem or threat to (white) British society. Similarly, in television comedy, minorities are often presented as objects of ridicule, for example because of the way they speak. 5

Item B

According to Marx, the class that owns and controls the means of material production – that is, the factories, offices, land, raw materials, transport, etc. needed for the production and distribution of goods and services – also controls the production and distribution of *ideas* in society. The ruling class is able to spread its ideas throughout society. As Marx put it, the ruling ideas in any society are the ideas of the ruling class. The ruling class is thus able to rule through ideas rather than through using force. It does this by creating and spreading *ideology* – ideas and beliefs which justify its position as the ruling class and the subordination of the working class and other groups. 5

Marxists argue that ruling-class ideology is to be found in all the institutions of capitalist society, such as the family, education system, and religion. In the case of the mass media, they argue that the media's output is inevitably ideological and serves the interests of the ruling class. 10

(a) What is meant by content analysis (**Item A, line 1**)? [2 marks]

(b) Suggest **two** criticisms of the use of content analysis in studying the mass media. [4 marks]

(c) Name **three** concepts that sociologists might use in explaining the production of news by the mass media. [6 marks]

(d) Identify and briefly explain **two** reasons why the mass media may have little or no direct influence on their audiences. [8 marks]

(e) Using material from **Item A** and elsewhere, examine the ways in which ethnicity is represented in the mass media. [20 marks]

(f) Using material from **Item B** and elsewhere, assess the view that the output of the mass media is inevitably ideological. [20 marks]

Examiner's hints

● In (e), note that 'ways' is plural. You can look at different media (television, press, etc.) and forms (soaps, news, adverts, etc.). You need to know some studies (e.g. Hall, Alvarado, Hartmann and Husband) and to be aware of variations in how ethnicity is represented.

● The view in (f) is usually associated with Marxism. Be clear what ideology means and consider different views as to why and how the media's output is ideological. Look at different varieties of Marxism (e.g. Gramsci, Marcuse, GUMG, etc.). Non-Marxist approaches (e.g. pluralism) could be used to evaluate the view.

Answers can be found on pages 82–84.

Item A

The Marxist view of education starts from the idea that in capitalist society, all social institutions, such as the family, religion, the mass media and so on, exist to serve the interests of the ruling class and to maintain the system of exploitation on which capitalism is based. In the view of most Marxists, this is also the basic role or purpose of the education system. For example, according to the American Marxist writers,   5 Bowles and Gintis, the education system performs two essential functions for capitalism. Firstly, it performs a *legitimation* function, legitimating the capitalist system, in particular through what they describe as 'the myth of meritocracy'.

Secondly, Bowles and Gintis argue that schooling performs a *reproduction* function. That is, it reproduces the existing class inequalities of capitalist society. According to   10 Bowles and Gintis, one way in which this occurs is through the working of the 'correspondence principle'. By this they mean that what goes on in school corresponds to or mirrors what takes place in work, thereby preparing pupils for a future as exploited wage-slaves.

Item B

There is now considerable evidence from sociological studies showing that members of different ethnic groups receive systematically different treatment in schools. This is not just the result of deliberate discrimination by individual teachers, however, but more importantly because of the systematic labelling of members of some minority groups using racist stereotypes. For example, Asian girls are more likely to be   5 stereotyped as passive and submissive, while Afro-Caribbean boys are more likely to be labelled as disruptive, and to be seen as good at sport or music rather than at subjects such as English and mathematics. Such labelling may have a serious negative effect on pupils' self-image and confidence.

Ethnocentric assumptions may also be part of the curriculum, so that the knowledge   10 that the school teaches and values reflects the culture of the white majority but not that of non-white minorities.

REBECCA'S ANSWER

(a) Explain what is meant by 'legitimation' (**Item A, line 7**). [2 marks]

Legitimation means to make something seem fair. Education makes inequality seem fair by making people think it's their own fault if they fail.

 2/2

(b) Give **two** examples of the 'correspondence principle' (**Item A, line 12**). [4 marks]

One example is the idea that school and work are both fragmented – into different subjects (at school), or into many small routine jobs at work (division of labour).

A second example of the correspondence principle is failure – the working class fail in school and at work.

 2/4

(c) Suggest **three** reasons why children from working-class backgrounds tend to do less well in school than those from middle-class backgrounds. [6 marks]

One reason is that working-class parents lack the resources of the middle class to pay for extra tuition, educational visits and toys etc.

Secondly, working-class children may only speak what Bernstein calls 'restricted code' which isn't useful for success.

Thirdly, the middle class gain an advantage at school by speaking the 'elaborated code' that the school, teachers etc. use and so they succeed.

 4/6

(d) Identify and briefly explain **two** criticisms of the Marxist view of the role of education in society. [8 marks]

One criticism is that the Marxist approach is too deterministic (structural view) to be true.

A second criticism often made is that because it is only concerned with how education reproduces capitalism and class, it ignores other sorts of social inequality. For example, it doesn't give much attention to how education reproduces gender or ethnic divisions.

 6/8

(a) Rebecca gives a **clear explanation** of the term. Her second sentence is exactly what the 'myth of meritocracy' is about – the myth that everyone has the same chance of success, so they believe it's their own fault, not capitalism's, if they fail.

(b) Rebecca understands what the correspondence principle is about – the mirroring of features of work by those of school. Her first example is spot on, but **her second reason is very weak** and does not score. A much better example she could have used is the idea that there is **hierarchy both in schools and at work**.

(c) Rebecca's first reason is fine: middle-class children enjoy **material advantages** over working-class children. Her second reason is also a good one: working-class children may not **speak the same 'language'** as their teachers. But her third reason is really the **same point put in a different way** and so it does not gain her any further marks.

(d) Rebecca doesn't quite make the full marks here because, although she **identifies** two criticisms, she only **explains** one of them. To get full marks, she needs to explain what determinism is and how this applies to the Marxist view of education. She could have said that it ignores the idea that pupils don't always do as capitalism requires them – e.g. they sometimes rebel instead of conforming to meet capitalism's needs.

Don't forget ...

When asked for a number of **different points**, don't make the mistake of simply re-stating the same one in different terms – as Rebecca did in question (c).

When you're revising a particular theory or study (such as Bowles and Gintis for example), make sure you try to learn at least **a couple of major criticisms** of it at the same time. Test yourself by trying to explain them clearly to a friend.

Evaluation is about strengths as well as weaknesses.

(e) Examine the reasons for the improvement in girls' educational achievements in recent years. [20 marks]

REBECCA'S ANSWER

In recent years females have been improving in terms of education. The girls have been outperforming the boys and there are several reasons for this. The introduction of coursework in many subjects is very significant. It has been claimed that girls are more suited to coursework and therefore they gain higher marks in it. They spend longer perfecting it whilst boys are more impatient.

> **Good point about coursework – different assessment methods may favour one gender or the other. But say *why* girls are more patient.**

Also feminism has had a big impact on the achievement of girls. Women no longer wish to stay at home and let their husbands go to work but instead they have altered their goals to become wage earners. Sue Sharpe, who carried out her study 'Just Like A Girl' in 1976 found that, at this time, the main priorities for girls were 'marriage, family, love, happiness and work' in roughly that order. However, when she repeated her study in the 1990s, she found that these priorities had changed. Girls now put career first and marriage last on their agenda.

> **Another good reason – backed up by Sharpe's studies. But Rebecca could look at why feminism has become important.**

Not only this but in school it is claimed that girls concentrate more and put much more effort into their work than the boys.

> **Very brief! She needs to explain *why* girls work harder – and maybe link it to the previous paragraph.**

Stanworth and Spender both found in their studies that teachers gave much more attention to boys in the class than to girls. This can be because boys are more disruptive than girls, so the teacher finds it harder to ignore them. Also, Stanworth found that teachers in an FE college were more likely to see girls' futures in traditional housewife/mother roles, even when they were more able than the boys.

> **Interesting, but not applied to the question: how does the fact that teachers ignore or stereotype girls explain why their performance has *improved*?**

However, we cannot ignore the fact that boys may now be underachieving, due to several factors. Boys spend less time on their work and tend to rush to finish it. It is claimed that they have a shorter concentration span and that they are lazier. Not only this but boys tend to spend more time out of the classroom due to misbehaviour and therefore they miss more of the work.

> **This loses sight of the idea of *change* that the question focuses on. Is she saying boys have suddenly become lazier or worse behaved? She gives no evidence for this.**

All of these factors are contributing to the rise in girls' educational achievement.

> **So brief it's hardly worth the bother! And does her previous paragraph say anything about girls anyway?**

10/20

Make sure you **interpret material in ways that make it relevant** to the question. Rebecca does this with her material on coursework and on Sharpe, but not on Stanworth and Spender, for example.

This question is about how and why girls' performance has improved, so you need to **focus on factors causing it to change over time**. As Stanworth's and Spender's studies both pre-date the improvement in girls' results, they don't directly explain the change. One way to interpret older material like this can be to say that the problems they raised (e.g. lack of teachers' attention to girls) have now been dealt with (e.g. through equal opportunities training for teachers).

The focus of the question is on **girls** – don't be drawn too far into discussing **boys**' achievements (or lack of them!). In any case, if boys' laziness or misbehaviour hasn't changed, then this doesn't really explain much.

Some **facts on girls' achievements** would be nice. You don't need to cram your head with statistics, but some indication that you know about trends at GCSE, AS/A level, SATs, or entry to HE would show that you realise girls are improving across the board. Likewise, something about **subject choice** would be good: girls might be doing better at exams, but are they still doing only the 'traditional' subjects?

There are **many other possible factors and explanations**. There have been many **changes within education**, such as the introduction of the National Curriculum (equal access to all subjects), league tables (schools now need girls to do better), and equal opportunities initiatives to encourage girls to achieve or take up non-traditional subjects.

Changes outside school, in wider society, are also important – such as changes **in the family** (more usually female-headed, lone parents) or **at work** (more women in paid work), changes **in the economy** (more jobs in 'female' occupations), equal opportunities **legislation**, **media** images of career women etc. You could discuss how these have affected girls' attitude to education (e.g. via the career aspirations Sharpe refers to).

Try to use some relevant **sociological theory** to help explain the changes. For example, different varieties of **feminism**, or the **functionalist** concept of meritocracy, could be relevant here.

Don't forget ...

Questions often ask you to examine the reasons for something. **Aim to identify at least four or five main reasons** and give yourself a paragraph on each of them.

Introduce some theories or perspectives to help make sense of the reasons from a sociologist's viewpoint. In general, you need to be familiar with functionalism, Marxism, interactionism and feminism, though you don't always need all of these in any one question!

(f) Using material from **Item B** and elsewhere, assess the view that children from ethnic minorities under-achieve in education because of discrimination and stereotyping in schools. [20 marks]

REBECCA'S ANSWER

As Item B suggests, ethnic minority pupils under-achieve because of stereotyping and discrimination at school. Because of their working-class background, they are often seen by teachers as 'slow learners'. This label then colours the teachers' view of all ethnic groups and therefore when an ethnic child goes to school he/she is given a negative label. Once the child starts to take on this label and sees himself in terms of it becomes a self-fulfilling prophecy, i.e. he becomes what the label said he was (e.g. no good at academic subjects) and so he fails. This is an interactionist view because it stresses how negative labels and interactions with teachers etc. affect minority pupils.

The Swann Report found that these labels and stereotypes are maintained through things like teaching materials and the curriculum. For example, it was found that history really meant British or white history, so as to say that black or Asian people didn't really have any history before the British arrived in their countries. This is called the ethnocentric curriculum, and it is a kind of message to pupils about who is superior or inferior.

This is similar to girls or working-class children being told that they are inferior to boys or to the middle class. For example, if music lessons are about classical music, it is likely that this is what middle-class pupils and parents listen to at home, so the school is saying that middle-class musical tastes are better and working-class ones are no good, probably leading to working-class pupils not achieving as well in the subject.

Ethnic minorities also under-achieve because of home background. They are more likely to be working class, so they under-achieve for the same reasons as white working-class people, e.g. poverty, unemployment, bad housing etc. may lead to failure. Also, as minorities often live in poor inner city areas, they are more likely to go to bad schools.

So as we can see the main reason for under-achievement by ethnic minorities is due to schools and teachers discriminating by labelling them negatively, but there are also home background factors like poverty or language and cultural attitudes to consider.

12/20

Quite a good explanation of labelling as applied to ethnicity. Rebecca could refer to a relevant study of labelling and ethnicity here.

Good material on the curriculum. She could introduce the idea of the *hidden* curriculum too.

Rebecca is right to point out the similarities between class and ethnicity in terms of the curriculum, but she loses focus on the question. More relevant material on ethnicity and stereotyping or discrimination would be better.

Rebecca rightly raises some 'outside school' causes of under-achievement. She could develop these points further and she should use them to evaluate the view in the question.

A reasonable conclusion – but she shouldn't leave it until the last line to bring up language and cultural attitudes!

How to score full marks

The question refers to **'ethnic minorities' (plural)**, but Rebecca makes no attempt to look at different minorities. They **don't all have the same level of achievement**, and there are also **differences within** minority groups, for example based on class and gender. Remember, many children from minorities 'over'-achieve compared with the average.

Rebecca refers to **'ethnic'** children in her first paragraph. This term is meaningless, since all children have an ethnicity. She means 'ethnic **minority**' (or perhaps majority). Many people also consider the term offensive. For both these reasons, it should be avoided.

Rebecca rightly makes some **use of the Item**, but she has only one named study. You don't have to remember a telephone directory full of names, but you should be able to **describe the relevant points from two or three studies** in a question such as this. For example, you could use **Wright**, **Gillborn**, **Mac an Ghaill**, **Fuller** or **Coard**.

'Assess' questions involve the skill of **evaluation**. Try to use your material on other explanations (such as home background factors) to discuss the **strengths and weaknesses** of the view in the question. You could also criticise the view by using **Fuller's** study of Afro-Caribbean girls' rejection of teachers' labels, also noting that not all minorities under-achieve.

Bring **other perspectives**, apart from interactionism, into the evaluation. Functionalists and the New Right generally blame the individual and their culture or background for failure, rather than the school.

You could introduce the impact of teacher training and anti-racism courses on teachers' attitudes.

Don't forget ...

Use the Item whenever the question tells you to. If you don't, you stand no chance of scoring the highest marks.

Questions on **ethnicity** – whether in education or other areas like work, family etc. – expect you to be aware that there are differences both within and between ethnic groups. Make some reference to these in your answer. Don't make the mistake of lumping all minorities together!

Key points to remember

The role of the education system: Most of the approaches to this issue take a 'macro' view: they look at society as a whole and how education 'fits in' to it. **Functionalists** take a positive view of the education system. They argue that it performs vital functions for society. It is an agency of secondary socialisation transmitting society's shared culture to the next generation and integrating them into society. It operates on meritocratic principles, selecting and allocating individuals on the basis of ability to different roles in the economy, with the most able getting the highest rewards. **Marxists** take a highly critical view of the education system. They see it as transmitting ruling-class ideology, persuading the working class to accept their position in capitalist society. For example, belief in meritocracy legitimates the individual's position in the hierarchy. They see education as reproducing the class structure, turning out sufficient numbers of different kinds of worker to meet the needs of capitalism. Marxists such as Willis see this happening in a contradictory way: working-class pupils rebel against school, forming their own social class-based subculture – but their very rejection of the school's values ensures they will fail and be destined for working-class jobs. Many **feminists** have also argued that education serves to maintain women's dependence and subordination, or to prepare boys and girls for their gender roles. **New Right thinkers** argue that the education system and its curriculum should become more responsive to the needs of the economy, equipping pupils for work and contributing to national economic efficiency.

Differential educational achievement: Pupils of different social groups achieve unequally. On average, middle class do better than working class, girls now out-perform boys, and children of some ethnic groups, such as whites and Indians, do better than Afro-Caribbeans, Pakistanis and Bangladeshis. Sociologists put forward many different explanations for why some groups are less successful. Some argue that they are the result of **factors outside the school**. These include material factors such as poverty, overcrowding, poor nutrition and lack of resources for educational equipment, etc. They also include cultural factors such as inappropriate socialisation, inadequate language skills or restricted speech code. In the case of ethnic minorities, racism also restricts opportunities and compounds disadvantages. For girls, it is argued that changes in the economy (more job opportunities for women) and the family (more divorces and lone mothers) may encourage girls to achieve at school. However, many sociologists argue that **relationships and processes within schools** also play a key role in producing these patterns of unequal achievement.

Relationships and processes within schools: Most of the sociologists interested in this issue take a 'micro' view. For example, **interactionists** focus on small-scale, classroom interactions. They explain differences in achievement in terms of concepts like labelling and the self-fulfilling prophecy. Teachers negatively stereotype working-class children and ethnic minorities, who internalise these labels and act them out. Interactionists also note the formation of anti-school subcultures among pupils sharing negative labels. Their adoption of anti-school values gives them an alternative source of status but leads to their failure, thus fulfilling the prophecy of their label. Other processes within schools include **streaming, banding and setting**. These also involve labelling or classifying groups of pupils as more able, less able etc. Sociologists have also emphasised the importance of the **hidden curriculum** – the ideas, beliefs and values that pupils learn alongside the official curriculum.

Government education policies: These determine the framework within which education takes place – for example, whether all pupils will go to the same kind of secondary school (the comprehensive system) or to different kinds depending on whether they pass or fail their eleven-plus exam (the tripartite system of grammar, technical and secondary modern schools, each with a different curriculum). Other policies, such as compensatory education, 'league tables', parental choice, the National Curriculum or allowing schools to 'opt out' of local authority control, all have an effect on pupils' experience of education and may affect achievement. For example, middle-class parents may be better placed to 'choose' a school with good results than working-class parents.

Item A

The value of the functionalist approach to education lies mainly in the emphasis that it gives to the links between the education system and aspects of the wider social structure. In particular, by highlighting the links between education and the economy, functionalism has ensured that the process of selection and differentiation within schools, and the distribution of rewards which result from these processes, have become key issues of sociological interest.

5

Item B

Some explanations of class differences in educational attainment adopt a 'micro' sociological framework, turning inwards to look at the internal workings of schools. Two areas of the schooling process and pupils' experience of it have received particular attention from interactionist sociologists: streaming (banding or setting) and teachers' expectations.

5

Another important aspect of the schooling process is the hidden curriculum – all the unofficial or informal learning that takes place inside schools. Sociologists argue that through the hidden curriculum, educational success and failure are socially constructed. It has also been argued that the curriculum is ethnocentric, and that this adversely affects the attainment of pupils from ethnic minority backgrounds.

10

(a) Explain what is meant by 'streaming'. [2 marks]

(b) Give **two** examples of ways in which the school curriculum may be seen as ethnocentric. [4 marks]

(c) Suggest **three** ways in which schools act as agencies of socialisation. [6 marks]

(d) Identify and briefly explain **two** reasons why females in general are now achieving better GCSE grades than males. [8 marks]

(e) Explain how the hidden curriculum and processes within schools help to produce inequalities between children of different social classes. [20 marks]

(f) Using material from **Item A** and elsewhere, assess the contribution of functionalist sociologists to an understanding of the role of education in society. [20 marks]

Examiner's hints
- For (e), remember that the question is asking about social class – don't drift off into gender or ethnicity. Remember, too, that you are being asked to look at *both* the hidden curriculum *and* processes within schools. You need to look especially at interactionist concepts, such as labelling, the self-fulfilling prophecy, streaming, and pupil subcultures, since these focus on what goes on within schools.
- For (f), you could focus on two key roles that functionalists see education playing: promoting social solidarity through socialisation into a shared culture, and selecting and allocating individuals meritocratically for roles in the division of labour. Remember, too, to evaluate the functionalist view by considering criticisms, especially from a Marxist perspective.

Answers can be found on pages 85–87.

Item A

Mack and Lansley used a democratic or consensual definition of poverty. In a survey of 1174 people in 1983, they presented their respondents with a list of 35 items and asked them to choose those items that they thought necessities. Over 90 per cent of respondents said that heating, an indoor toilet and a bath (not shared with another household), a damp-free home, and beds for everyone were necessities. Over two-thirds of respondents also included items such as three meals a day for children, a warm waterproof coat, enough money for public transport, two pairs of all-weather shoes, a refrigerator, toys for children, carpets, a roast joint or similar once a week, a washing machine, and celebrations on special occasions such as Christmas. 5

Altogether, there were 22 items which over half the respondents deemed to be necessities. Mack and Lansley defined as poor anyone who lacked three or more of these items because they could not afford them. On this basis, they calculated that in 1983 about 7.5 million people were in poverty. 10

Mack and Lansley carried out a follow-up study in 1990. They found that the public's perceptions of necessities had changed. For example, more people now thought a fridge essential (92 per cent, as against 77 per cent in 1983). 15

Item B

Over 80 per cent of Pakistani and Bangladeshi households have below average incomes as against only 28 per cent of white households. At the other extreme, 23 per cent of white households have incomes above one and a half times the national average income, but only one per cent of Pakistani households have incomes this high.

Women make up about two-thirds of the adults in the poorest households. One million more women than men are in poverty. 5

58 per cent of lone parents are poor, but only 24 per cent of couples with children and only 13 per cent of couples without children.

26 per cent of pensioner couples and 35 per cent of single pensioners are poor.

47 per cent of disabled people live in poverty. 10

TOM'S ANSWER

(a) What is meant by a 'democratic or consensual definition of poverty' (**Item A, line 1**)? [2 marks]

'Consensus' means agreement. A consensual definition of poverty is one which is agreed by most people (which is also what democracy involves — majority agreement/rule). A definition of poverty shared by most of society.

 2/2

(b) Suggest **two** criticisms of the idea of absolute poverty. [4 marks]

One criticism is that absolute definitions of poverty assume that everyone has the same basic needs, which is not true. A building worker needs more calories than an office worker, because he does a heavy manual job, meaning he uses up much more energy fulfilling his role. Also it is likely that building workers and office workers will have different non-basic needs as well, e.g. they will probably have different leisure needs etc. 2/4

(c) Name **three** sources of welfare for individuals other than the state. [6 marks]

1 Private health care.
2 Local authorities provide welfare, e.g. meals on wheels for the disabled.
3 Charities, e.g. Age Concern, provide help for the elderly. 4/6

(d) Identify and briefly explain **two** criticisms that could be made of the research described in **Item A**. [8 marks]

One criticism is that their definition of poverty isn't really a democratic or consensual one, because the public didn't really choose the necessities — they only chose from a list that the researchers had drawn up for them. What if the public had wanted to include other things that they thought were necessities? This wouldn't have been possible — they could only pick from what was there.

Another problem is that if you add extra items to the list of necessities when you repeat the research, then you won't be able to make a true comparison over time, since poverty at one time will be a lack of one set of things and at another time it will be a lack of a different set of things. Not comparing like with like.

 8/8

How to score full marks

(a) A good answer. Mack and Lansley's approach was to ask the public what they thought were necessities and so arrive at **the public's shared definition of poverty**.

(b) Tom's first reason is a good one: absolute definitions assume that there is **a single fixed minimum** standard of living needed for physical health and efficiency, yet as Tom notes, people with different jobs will have **different** food needs. However, Tom's second point, about 'non-basic needs', doesn't score, because the idea of absolute poverty is based on the idea of **basic** needs. Tom might have done better to separate·out his two points – it might have helped him spot that the second one was wrong.

(c) Tom gets the first source right: any **private** welfare – i.e. **provided for profit by a company or business** – would do, such as private education, private insurance for unemployment etc. However, he gets the second one wrong – **local** authorities (or local government) are just as much part of the state as are **central** government departments such as the Department of Social Security. Tom's third source – **charities** – is also right. He could also have chosen **informal welfare providers**, such as friends, family or neighbours.

(d) Two very good criticisms, well explained, so full marks here.

Don't forget ...

When asked to make more than one point, it's a good idea to **separate them out by numbering them** (firstly, secondly, etc.) or starting each point on a new line.

Be clear about **basic concepts** such as different definitions of poverty and learn some **criticisms** and some **examples** of each concept.

(e) Explain why some sociologists argue that the welfare state has failed to help the poor. [20 marks]

TOM'S ANSWER

The welfare state was set up in the 1940s after the Second World War by the Labour government. Its aim was to eradicate poverty, bad housing, bad health, etc. However, many sociologists think that it has failed to help those who need it, i.e. the poor.

New Right thinkers argue that poverty is the fault of the poor themselves but that the welfare state makes this worse, for example by giving council flats to teenage single mothers. Charles Murray (US sociologist) calls this 'perverse incentives', i.e. the state is rewarding 'bad' behaviour, so encouraging the problem to grow. If young girls know they will get a flat if they get pregnant, some will do so — e.g. to escape their parents' authority. This then means they won't be able to work and will live off benefit.

The New Right solution is to cut the welfare state back. It seems that they think that the less the state does for the poor the more it will in fact be helping them. This is because they will learn to get out of their culture of dependency and stand on their own feet.

Some sociologists don't really look at the welfare state in their explanation of why poverty exists. For example, the culture of poverty thesis is put forward by Lewis. He argues that the poor create a subculture of 'live for today' to help them cope with poverty, unskilled labour, etc. The trouble is that when opportunities do arise to get out of poverty, the poor are too 'adapted' to it to change their ways.

Marxists think that the welfare state is part of capitalism and works to benefit the ruling class, e.g. the National Health Service patches up workers so they can keep working to make profits for the bourgeoisie.

Feminists think that the welfare state benefits men not women (though some of them e.g. Marxist feminists think it serves the ruling class rather than working-class men). This is why women are more likely to be in poverty — the welfare state keeps them trapped there.

Good idea to contrast why the welfare state was set up with what it has actually achieved for the poor. But some sociologists claim its aim was to manage poverty, not eradicate it – so better to say 'Some say its aim was ...'.

Good – the New Right blame the welfare state for creating poverty, not reducing it. Useful example, too.

Tom builds on the previous paragraph, but could explain 'culture of dependency' and maybe mention the underclass.

Tom's first sentence gives the game away – this paragraph isn't really relevant. He's drifted into a general 'explanations of poverty' answer, unlinked to the question.

Potentially, a very useful paragraph, but needs further explanation. Also, Tom's example is about health, not poverty.

Again, relevant to the question, but needs more. An example or two would be good.

> **A conclusion of sorts, but to a slightly different question. He could end with a contrast as to why New Right, Marxists etc. think it has failed the poor.**

So although some sociologists think the welfare state has failed to help the poor, others explain poverty as the fault of a culture of poverty.

12/20

How to score full marks

Tom shows a **fairly good knowledge but he doesn't always apply it**. For example, he knows about the culture of poverty, but doesn't find a way to link it to the question – probably because it's quite hard to do so. However, he might be able to make a connection to the welfare state via the idea of 'opportunities' provided by the education system (a part of the welfare state).

Develop your points. Tom has a short paragraph on Marxism, which is potentially very useful for this question, but it needs taking further. For example, though he identifies the Marxist view of the welfare state correctly (it serves capitalism), you could develop this by spelling out the Marxist idea that the welfare state maintains the poor as a **reserve army of labour** on low benefit levels **to keep down wages** of those in work.

The same is true for his paragraph on feminism. Concepts like **patriarchy**, **enforced dependence on men**, etc. could be used. Examples from the **benefits system** could be used to illustrate this dependence. Tom has a good example for the New Right view (pregnant teenagers), so why not find one for feminism?

Write **a sharper, more focused conclusion** than Tom did. He seems to be summing up an answer to a more general question: 'What causes poverty – is it the state or not?' (This also explains the section on Lewis.) You could end by **comparing and contrasting** some of the views dealt with earlier – New Right versus Marxist would be good: radical right wing versus radical left wing approaches. Both criticise the welfare state for failing to solve the problem of poverty, but for different reasons.

Don't forget ...

Avoid writing 'All I know about poverty (or whatever other topic)' answers. You probably know quite a lot (hopefully!), but you have to show the examiner **you know what's relevant to the question**.

Leave time to check that each sentence adds something to your answer to the set question – not to the question you would have set!

(f) Using material from **Item B** and elsewhere, assess sociological explanations of why some groups are at greater risk of poverty than others.

[20 marks]

TOM'S ANSWER

Good idea to start with the Item – the question tells him to use it. Might be an idea to say *which explanations* will be looked at.

Good point about power and status but he should develop it. Useful examples.

Starts off OK, but doesn't show how individualistic explanations explain groups' poverty. 'Structural constraints' point hints at evaluation but needs explaining.

Good – he outlines the underclass approach and then criticises it, with a relevant example about disability.

Good – Tom debates different causes of poverty among minorities: racism at work, language, qualifications – and racism again. Well reasoned and uses Item and other evidence.

As Item B shows, some groups are more likely to find themselves in poverty, such as ethnic minorities, women, the old etc. For example, lone parents are more than twice as likely as couples with children to be poor. There can be a range of reasons for this pattern.

Some sociologists argue that poverty is due to some groups being less powerful or lower status than others. Men are more powerful than women, holding most of the important jobs etc. Disabled people have little power and are discriminated against, like black people.

Other sociologists argue that it is to do with these groups themselves. These are sometimes called victim-blaming explanations because they say that the poor (the victims of poverty) are to blame for their plight. The individualistic explanation says it is the fault of the individual for being lazy, unambitious, wasting their resources, etc. But this ignores the structural constraints that face the poor so they can't escape poverty.

Another explanation is the underclass. This argues that some groups like single parents have a culture of depending on others i.e. on the state, and this is why they are poor, whereas more 'respectable' groups (e.g. married couples) strive to provide for their families without looking for handouts. In other words, the underclass groups (which also include many unemployed as well as petty criminals, etc.) are poor because they prefer to live that way. However, this doesn't explain why some others are poor such as the disabled. For example, a person might be hard working but have an accident at work (more likely for manual workers) and become disabled.

Ethnic minorities are often poorer than whites, as Item B shows. This can be because of racism and discrimination by employers and others, preventing minorities from getting work (many minorities have higher rates of unemployment) or promotion. On the other hand, it can also be because of language and educational barriers — e.g. many Pakistanis and Bangladeshis may not speak very good English and they have below average educational qualifications. However, this may also be due partly to discrimination and racism, for example the Swann Report into the education of minorities found that many teachers were unconsciously racist, so this affects the chances of these pupils to get good qualifications and well-paid jobs that will keep them out of poverty.

A quick summary of explanations, plus a reasonable point to end on.

In general, there are a variety of explanations for why some groups are poorer than others, such as the individualistic explanation, structural and victim-blaming views, discrimination, language, etc. Perhaps there is no single explanation for all of them and we need different ones for different groups.

14/20

How to score full marks

Overall, this is a good answer. Tom looks at **a range of different groups**. He **uses the Item**, as required by the question, and he puts forward **a number of different explanations**. He also **begins to evaluate** some of the material that he uses. However, there is still room for improvement!

Lots of useful concepts, but some need further development. Tom could discuss **power and status** further – Max Weber could be brought in here. Likewise, **structural constraints** could be explained and applied.

Look for ways to **bring in theories** (like Weber, above). **Marxists, feminists, functionalists, the New Right** (to name but a few!) all have explanations of why some groups are poor. For instance, **functionalists** may explain poverty in terms of some of these **groups not sharing mainstream achievement-oriented values** (recent immigrants, perhaps). The **New Right** could be linked to Tom's **'underclass' paragraph**.

Most of Tom's material is relevant, but the point about **individualistic explanations** doesn't work very well and should be cut out or **thought through for a link** to 'groups'.

What gets you **high marks on 'assess' questions** is showing the examiner that you can **evaluate**. Here, you need to evaluate different explanations. You can do this in various ways – e.g. by giving **evidence or arguments for or against** an explanation, like Tom's point about accidents at work, or by using **information from the Item** (like his example of Bangladeshis and Pakistanis), or by **comparing or contrasting it** with other views.

Don't forget ...

Make concepts work for you. If you know a concept is relevant, spell out its meaning and explain why you're using it.

Link reasons and concepts to theoretical explanations – e.g. link 'underclass' to 'New Right'. Then discuss the theory!

Who are the poor? Some groups of people are more likely to be poor than others: the unemployed, the low paid, the unskilled (often the same people), ethnic minorities, the elderly, households with children (especially lone parents), the disabled. One reason is that these groups are **excluded from paid work**, or have insecure jobs, and thus depend on state benefits.

Defining and measuring poverty: Sociologists disagree on what poverty is. Some favour an **absolute** definition: poverty is a lack of basic necessities to meet physical needs. Official benefit levels are based largely on a subsistence or absolute view of poverty. Other sociologists prefer a **relative** definition, seeing poverty as a lack of those things that others in society take for granted.

The higher the income level at which the poverty line is drawn, the more people will fall underneath it and so the greater the numbers in poverty. Whether poverty still exists in today's society is a political as well as a sociological issue. Conservative or **right-wing views** tend to favour an absolute definition of poverty and to see it as all but wiped out. Marxists and social democrats, with **left-wing views**, favour a relative definition that links poverty to inequality (which they are against), and argue that poverty still persists.

Wealth and income: Wealth is a **stock** of assets or resources (e.g. savings and investments, property etc.), while income is a **flow** of resources (e.g. wages, interest on savings, dividends on shares, or rent received from property leased to others). **Income is unequally distributed** – some earn far more than others, some have large unearned income from investments, and tax cuts over the last 20 years mean that the rich now keep a higher proportion of their income. But **wealth is more unequally distributed** – in 1996, 1% of the population owned 19% of all wealth, while the poorest 50% owned only 7% of the total. **Functionalists** argue that income inequality is functional since the most important jobs can be most highly rewarded, thereby motivating individuals to strive for these positions, to the benefit of all. However, **Marxists** argue that in capitalist society, massive inequalities in wealth concentrate power in the hands of a minority ruling class who inherit rather than achieve their privileged position.

Explanations of poverty: Non-sociological **individualistic** theories argue that the cause of poverty lies in the failings of individuals, e.g. as a result of their laziness. By contrast, all sociological theories of poverty argue that the cause lies in some aspect of society, rather than in individuals. Some theories argue that poverty is the result of the **subculture of the poor**. For example, Oscar Lewis argues the shared norms and values that enable the poor to cope with a life of hardship become a barrier to them escaping poverty. The New Right share this view, but see many of the poor as an **underclass** with a **culture of dependency** on state welfare. Other sociological theories, such as the Marxist view, argue that poverty is the result of the **unequal structure** of society, which traps some in poverty and permits them to be exploited by others.

Solutions to poverty: Can the problem of poverty be solved and, if so, how? Can the state be used to tackle the problem? Different perspectives give different answers. **Political liberals** (e.g. Beveridge, whose 1944 report laid the framework for the welfare state) believe that the state can provide a safety net for people's **welfare**. **Social democrats** such as Townsend go further, believing that the **state** can introduce a more equal society, gradually abolishing poverty. On the other hand, some approaches believe that the state cannot solve the problem of poverty. The **New Right** argue that state welfare only creates dependence on handouts, reducing initiative and undermining economic prosperity. **Marxists** argue that as the state's purpose is to serve capitalism, it cannot solve the problem of poverty, since this is caused by capitalism. Feminists take the view that the state perpetuates male domination, so cannot free women from poverty.

Welfare providers: As well as the state or **public sector** (e.g. the NHS, social services, education, council housing and social security), there are other providers of welfare. Some of these are charities in the **voluntary sector** (e.g. Help the Aged). Others are businesses or profit-making bodies in the **private sector**. There is also an **informal sector** of friends, neighbours and relatives who look after the elderly, young children, the sick and disabled. Recent governments have favoured a policy of **care in the community**, shifting people out of institutions and into the 'community'.

Item A

Poverty is particularly a problem for women. Older people are more likely
to be living in poverty than other age groups, and older women are especially
vulnerable to poverty and necessity in all societies. In Britain in 1987, for
example, more than one older woman in three (35 per cent) was living on an
income at or below Supplementary Benefit level (now known as Income   5
Support), compared with a quarter of men. Older women living alone are even
more likely to be living in poverty – just under 50 per cent, compared with 40 per
cent of single older men. In 1988 three times as many older women as men were
living in households with below average incomes.

Source: adapted from P. Abbott and C. Wallace, *An Introduction to Sociology:*
Feminist Perspectives (Routledge, 2nd edition, 1997)

Item B

Explanations offered as to the causes of poverty are often divided into two main
types. The first type, 'individualistic' theories, identify the main causes of
poverty as being within the individuals themselves, or in the characteristics of the subculture
to which they belong. This approach tends, therefore, to place the
blame for poverty on the poor themselves. The idea of the poor as 'undeserving'   5
was popular in Victorian times, and echoes of that view can be found in the
writings of some commentators from the New Right today.

Sociologists supporting the second type of explanation see poverty as a product
of the structure of society itself, or of the inability of the Welfare State either to
prevent or to eradicate poverty. These 'structural' theories are predominantly advocated by   10
Marxists, but also by writers such as Gans, who believes that poverty exists because
it benefits the non-poor and therefore functions for society in general.

(a) Explain what is meant by the 'feminisation of poverty'. [2 marks]

(b) Identify **two** ways in which poverty may benefit the non-poor. [4 marks]

(c) Suggest how each of the following is a provider of welfare:

    (i) the state
    (ii) voluntary organisations
    (iii) the private sector. [6 marks]

(d) Identify and discuss **two** reasons why 'older women' are more likely to be in poverty than 'older men'. [8 marks]

(e) Examine some of the different ways that researchers have attempted to measure poverty. [20 marks]

(f) Using information from the **Items** and elsewhere, assess the usefulness of 'individualistic' theories of the causes of poverty. [20 marks]

Examiner's hints
- For (e), be aware of different studies of poverty – such as Rowntree, Townsend, Mack and Lansley etc. – and what measures they have used. Remember that problems of defining poverty are closely linked to problems of measuring it: what we think poverty is will affect how much of it we find when we come to measure it.
- For (f), remember that individualistic theories are non-sociological ones (like the 19th-century laissez-faire view) that look to the characteristics of individuals to explain why they are poor. You can criticise them from the standpoint of different sociological views, including both cultural and structural explanations of poverty.

Answers can be found on pages 88–90.

Exam Question and Answer

Item A

According to Marx, conflict at work is inevitable. In capitalist societies, two classes exist: on the one hand, there is a bourgeoisie or capitalist class of employers who own the means of production. On the other hand, there exists a working class or proletariat who own no means of production other than their own labour power, which they sell to the capitalist in exchange for a wage. However, this exchange is an unequal one and   5
the relationship between the two classes is one of exploitation. This exploitation, and the alienating conditions of work, make conflict inevitable.

Item B

In many ways, work is the most important of human activities. Without work being performed, we could not survive. Sociologists are interested in how work is organised, who controls it, who performs it, who benefits from it. They are interested in what effects work has on other aspects of our lives – for example, on leisure – and in the impact on individuals and society of unemployment. They are concerned with how   5
technology affects work: for example, do the new computerised information and communications technologies make work better or worse for workers?

SMITA'S ANSWER

(a) Explain what is meant by 'the means of production' (**Item A, line 3**). [2 marks]

The 'means of production' is for example things like factories etc. ½

(b) With reference to the new technologies described in **Item B**, suggest
   (i) **one** way in which they may make work **worse** for workers; [2 marks]
   (ii) **one** way in which they may make work **better** for workers. [2 marks]

One way they may make things worse is that they may mean you don't need as many workers to do a job, i.e. it will cause redundancies. 2/2

One way the new technologies may make things better is they will make products cheaper. 0/2

(c) Suggest **three** reasons why some workers may find their work alienating. [6 marks]

One reason is because it's very routine and repetitive.
Another reason is they are isolated from fellow workers
(e.g. on an assembly line, you can't move around and chat).
A third reason is that it may be boring. 4/6

(d) Identify and briefly describe **two** ways in which work affects leisure. [8 marks]

One way work affects leisure is by affecting a person's income.
For example, a manual worker is on a lower income than say a barrister, so he/she (the manual worker) wouldn't be able to afford things like belonging to private sports clubs/gyms.
A second way is that it affects the time you have for leisure. 6/8

Don't forget ...

When you're asked for an explanation, don't just give an example.

Check that you're not repeating yourself when you give a list of reasons or other points.

THE HENLEY COLLEGE LIBRARY

(a) When Smita says 'for example things like factories etc.', she's not really giving an explanation, only an example. **An explanation needs a definition** – such as this one: the means of production are **all those things needed or used in the production process**, including raw materials, machines, buildings, offices and human labour.

(b) Smita does fine on part (i) – one of the big fears many sociologists and members of the public have is that the benefits brought by the new technologies will be paid for by some **people losing their jobs**. Another answer would be: by giving employers greater powers of surveillance over workers. On part (ii), Smita doesn't show how **workers** might gain. A better answer might be that the new technologies may **take some of the drudgery out of work or enable workers to develop new skills**.

(c) The first two reasons are correct, **but the third one looks too much like the first to score**. Other valid answers could include: because workers don't own what they produce; because they have no say in how the work is organised or what product is produced (i.e. powerlessness); because they are estranged from their true self.

(d) Two good points identified – time and money. Unfortunately, although Smita describes how the first one affects leisure, **she doesn't develop the second point**. So four marks for the money, but only two for the time. She could have said that some people have to **work shifts or long hours and this restricts their leisure opportunities**.

(e) Examine the ways in which sociologists can help us to understand unemployment. [20 marks]

SMITA'S ANSWER

Unemployment is a very serious social problem and sociologists can help us to understand it better. There are different ways they can do this, e.g. by explaining the causes and also the effects on society.

Unemployment can be defined as not having a job. There are many reasons for this. For example, if you live in an inner-city area, businesses often don't want to set up there as there is too much crime. Also you might be working in an industry or business that closes down, like the coalmines back in the 1980s. This can be because of a government decision or other factors like competition from abroad, which can be the result of globalisation.

Some groups find it harder to get a job than others. According to the Rowntree Foundation, young black men find it harder to get a job than whites — this is even true for black graduates. This may be because of racial discrimination. Some sociologists say that many blacks are unemployed because they are part of the underclass, e.g. New Right sociologist Murray sees the poor as deliberately unemployed because they have a dependency culture, preferring to live off benefits.

Other groups also find it hard to keep or get jobs. These include school-leavers and older people, perhaps because of age discrimination. Unemployment can also have many bad effects on people, such as family breakdown and divorce. On the other hand, it can lead to role reversal in the marriage if unemployed men stay at home while their wives become the breadwinner. So we can see that sociologists can tell us numerous things about unemployment, i.e. its causes and effects, so that hopefully the government can do something to improve it.

10/20

A relevant start, but could mention one other way sociologists might help us understand unemployment: namely, the problem of how we define and measure it.

A quick definition, then into some causes. She would do better to spend more time on the issue of definition. Some relevant causes, though: area, government policy, globalisation – but could say more about the last point.

Smita deals with why some groups are more at risk than others, but she could also give alternative views to Murray's.

Some more 'at risk' groups identified, plus a possible cause. A little about effects, but she could say more.

How to score full marks

Smita suggests she's going to write about causes *and* effects, yet she only mentions the **effects** at the very end. You could develop this by discussing effects **on ill health, death (including suicide) rates, poverty, crime and disorder, extra social security and NHS costs, etc**.

You could also say more about **causes and groups at risk** than Smita does. Use the Marxist concept of **reserve army of labour** or the Weberian idea of **dual labour markets** to explain gender and ethnic differences in unemployment rates.

Smita skips over the issue of **definition and measurement**. This is an important aspect of the study of unemployment and it also **has links to 'Sociological Methods'**, where you could use it as an example of the problems of **official statistics**. What problems are there in relying on them to give us a picture of unemployment? You should discuss the **reliability and validity** of unemployment statistics.

Don't forget ...

Make a plan – and stick to it.

Concepts are central to a good answer.

Look for links and draw on your knowledge of other topics, such as 'Sociological Methods'.

(f) Using information from **Item A** and elsewhere, assess the view that conflict at work is inevitable. [20 marks]

SMITA'S ANSWER

The main form of conflict at work is strikes. According to Item A, Marxists argue that conflict at work is inevitable because of capitalism. Two classes exist — the capitalists (bourgeoisie) and the workers (proletariat). The workers don't own the means of production (factories) so they have to go and work for the capitalists for wages instead, but this leads to exploitation.

There are many different forms of conflict, such as work to rule or strikes. Strikes are when workers withdraw their labour to pursue some particular issue like a claim for more money. Other reasons for strikes are the threat of redundancies or, for instance, over the conditions of work, e.g. if these are dangerous or unhealthy, workers might go on strike to get them improved.

Talcott Parsons has a functionalist view of work. He argues that conflict at work doesn't exist, because of value consensus — everyone agrees about the need to work together. Pluralists think that there is some conflict but not major conflict, because everybody's interests are taken account of.

Conditions at work can cause conflict. If work is boring and monotonous, like in assembly-line work, this may cause grievances or workers may just go on strike to break the monotony. Work that is de-skilled is also going to be a source of conflict, because if your job is interesting you aren't going to want to be going out on strike all the time.

To conclude, therefore, we can say that some sociologists believe conflict is inevitable, namely the Marxists and also in certain kinds of work like assembly lines, whereas other sociologists such as Parsons do not believe there is much, if any, conflict at work. So whether it is inevitable all depends on what perspective you take.

9/20

Marxism is a reasonable place to start, but Smita doesn't really do much more than repeat some of the material in Item A. She needs to explain exploitation and link it to conflict.

Some potentially relevant points about causes of strikes. Work to rule briefly mentioned, but what about other forms of conflict? Also, she needs to link this information to the question of 'inevitability'.

Correct and relevant, but brief – Smita needs to explain these views further and show how they link to the question.

Might go better with second paragraph (about conditions). A valid point about boredom and de-skilling, but she needs some sociological context and concepts to link it to the question. And do workers with interesting jobs *never* go on strike?!

Smita attempts a conclusion, summing up the main points of the answer, but a weak one.

Smita tries to use the material from the Item, but she doesn't add anything new. **Look for ways to develop what you find in the Items**. For example, explain what Marxists mean by exploitation and why this leads to inevitable conflicts between workers and capitalists.

Know your stuff. Smita's knowledge of relevant material is a bit thin – some points about types of conflicts and causes of strikes, plus one paragraph on Parsons and pluralism. **Give more detail of these approaches** – e.g. explain why and how pluralists believe conflict can be minimised. Likewise, **bring in other forms of conflict**, such as lock-outs, sabotage, etc. You could also look at why some industries are more 'strike-prone' than others.

Make your points explicitly **relevant to the question**. With each paragraph, look for ways to tie the material to the issue of the **inevitability** of conflict.

'Assess the view' means you have to **evaluate**. You need to weigh up different views in terms of **arguments and evidence for or against** the Marxist, functionalist, pluralist or other approaches, and draw conclusions based on this. How convincing do you find each perspective's standpoint?

Don't forget ...

Make use of the Items, but **don't just restate them** – build on them with your own knowledge.

Don't say 'it all depends on what perspective you take' – it rarely does!

The management and organisation of work: Taylor's **Scientific Management** approach argued that there is one best way of organising any work task and that workers are motivated only by economic rewards. Management could raise productivity by selecting workers carefully and paying piece rates. Mayo's **Human Relations** approach stresses the importance of social needs and informal work groups. Henry Ford's car plants in the early twentieth century gave rise to the idea of **Fordism**: mass production of cheap, standardised products by assembly-line technology. **Marxists** like Braverman argue that capitalist mass production, with its intensive division of labour, de-skills and controls workers. **Post-Fordist** production involves using new information technology, flexible specialisation and a workforce divided into core and periphery.

Work satisfaction and alienation: Many workers gain little satisfaction from work. Sociologists refer to this experience as **alienation**. Marxists see it as the product of capitalism. Blauner sees alienation as the result of particular types of technology, especially assembly-line production. Goldthorpe and Lockwood's 'action' approach focuses on the meaning workers give to their work: well-paid assembly-line workers with an 'instrumental' attitude will not be dissatisfied with their work.

Technological changes and their impact: Sociologists are divided about the impact of new technology. Marxists tend to see it as just another way of **de-skilling** and controlling the workforce or making profits. Blauner and others see automated production as reducing alienation or raising skill levels. It may lead to new forms of work organisation, such as post-Fordism. It can raise productivity, create or destroy jobs, and is a major factor promoting globalisation.

Conflict: Conflict at work includes strikes, working to rule, sabotage, absenteeism, lock-outs and sackings. It can occur over pay, conditions, redundancy threats or alienation. **Marxists** argue that conflict is inevitable in capitalism. Different industries have different levels of conflict. Fear of unemployment and falling trade union membership have led to lower strike rates in recent years.

Unemployment: There are problems in **defining and measuring** unemployment. The definition is highly political: the Conservative government in the 1980s was accused of repeatedly redefining unemployment so as to reduce the official total. Unemployment statistics may also underestimate the real total, for example because unemployed married women who would not be eligible for benefit don't bother to register as unemployed. Structural **causes** of unemployment include changes in the occupational structure (e.g. the decline of manufacturing), new technology and globalisation leading to increased competition. Some groups are more at risk of unemployment, such as the unskilled, older workers and unqualified school-leavers. Discrimination against minorities also causes higher rates for some groups. New Right thinkers argue that many of the unemployed are members of the underclass whose 'dependency culture' prevents them seeking work. The **effects** of unemployment – often affecting whole communities – include poverty, higher sickness and death (including suicide) rates, family breakdown, crime and disorder, and welfare and policing costs.

Leisure: Sociologists have tried to explain why different groups have different leisure patterns. Marxists, feminists, pluralists and others have related leisure to factors such as occupation, social class, gender roles, family, age and ethnicity. More recently, sociologists influenced by postmodernism have seen leisure as an important aspect of **identity** and have studied the ways in which people actively use leisure to construct their identities through their consumption patterns.

Question to try

Item A

Although Roberts stresses the freedom of choice in leisure activities, he does not deny that social factors influence patterns of leisure. People choose to engage in leisure pursuits which fit in with their personal circumstances, life style and social group to which they belong. On the basis of his evidence, Roberts claims that work has relatively little influence on people's leisure pursuits. He points out that even   5 excluding the unemployed, about half of the population do not have paid work. For example, full-time housewives do not have their leisure influenced by work simply because they are not 'working'.

Source: adapted from M. Haralambos and M. Holborn,
Sociology: Themes and Perspectives, 4th edition (Collins Educational, 1995)

Item B

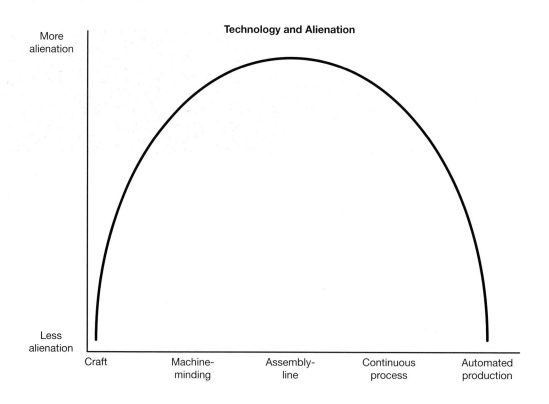

Source: adapted from R. Blauner, *Alienation and Freedom*
(University of Chicago Press, 1964)

(a) Explain what is meant by 'automated production' (**Item B**).

[2 marks]

(b) Suggest **two** factors which may influence a person's chance of being unemployed.

[4 marks]

(c) Suggest **three** ways in which patterns of work have changed over the last 25 years.

[6 marks]

(d) Identify and discuss **two** ways in which unemployment statistics may be misleading.

[8 marks]

(e) Using material from **Item A** and elsewhere, examine the influence of the role of work and other social factors on patterns of leisure.

[20 marks]

(f) Using material from **Item B** and elsewhere, assess sociological explanations of the nature and causes of alienation.

[20 marks]

Examiner's hints
- In part (e), remember to deal with 'other social factors' such as family, education, peer group, etc., not just different types of work.
- In part (f), you need to deal with more than one approach to alienation, such as Marx, Blauner and Goldthorpe and Lockwood. Use the Item to develop your account of Blauner and include criticisms of the explanations.

Answers can be found on pages 91–93.

Exam Question and Answer

Item A

Interactionist sociologists favour qualitative data. They seek to discover the meanings behind people's actions, and qualitative data gives an insight into the meanings which individual social actors attach to their own and each other's behaviour. For this reason, they prefer primary and secondary sources of data that allow them to 'get close' to the actor and their way of seeing the world. Such methods and sources include overt and   5
covert participant observation, unstructured interviews, life histories and diaries. According to interactionists, the great advantage of all of these is that they produce valid data. However, unlike quantitative methods and sources such as experiments and official statistics, it is said that methods like participant observation are not reliable and that they fail to produce representative data.   10

Item B

Sociologists in all countries are likely at one time or another to consult and draw on official statistics in their research. They are called 'official' as they are collected initially by government offices or departments for a range of reasons. Official statistics are used for a number of reasons, including the following:

● They are frequently the only available source of data in a particular area.   5

● They are readily available.

● They allow an examination of trends over time.

Despite these advantages, they do have a number of drawbacks, such as:

● They have been collected for a particular purpose, which has influenced how, when and for whom they were collected.   10

● The statistics are not 'objective' figures telling the 'real' story, but the end result of a complex process of social interaction. For example, crime statistics are the result of interactions between police, suspects, courts and others.

Source: adapted from T. Bilton et al., *Introductory Sociology*, 3rd edition (Macmillan, 1996)

PHIL'S ANSWER

(a) Name **one** type of official statistics other than that referred to in **Item B**. [2 marks]

Crime statistics.

 0/2

(b) Explain the difference between 'primary and secondary' sources of data (**Item A, line 4**). [4 marks]

Primary data refers to data that the researcher has gathered himself or herself, such as by using interviews. Secondary data is data from sources such as official statistics, diaries, letters or government reports.

 3/4

(c) Suggest **three** problems of using experiments in sociological research. [6 marks]

One problem would be that it's wrong to experiment on people without their knowledge/consent, yet if you tell them the true purpose of your experiment they may refuse to participate, or knowing what it's about might defeat the purpose of it.
Second, you can't fit the whole of society into a laboratory, so you couldn't study large-scale patterns and trends.
A lab. is an artificial environment — people wouldn't behave naturally, so your results may be invalid.

 6/6

(d) Identify and briefly describe **two** ethical problems which might face sociologists using covert participant observation. [8 marks]

One ethical problem is that you are deceiving people. Humphreys pretended to be a lookout when he was secretly observing male homosexual behaviour in public toilets for sociological purposes.
You are pretending to be someone else to get information that people wouldn't give you if they knew your true identity.
A second problem is that you may find yourself in danger.
If you pose as one of the gang and they find out that you are really an observer, they might attack you.

 4/8

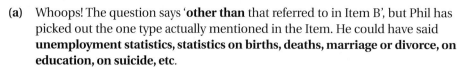

How to score full marks

(a) Whoops! The question says '**other than** that referred to in Item B', but Phil has picked out the one type actually mentioned in the Item. He could have said **unemployment statistics, statistics on births, deaths, marriage or divorce, on education, on suicide, etc**.

(b) Spot on as regards primary data – a clear explanation which gets 2 marks. Not quite enough on secondary data, though: although Phil seems to know what this kind of data is, he hasn't actually defined or explained the term, **merely given some examples** – so he only gets 1 of the 2 marks for this side of the question. A definition of secondary data is: data created or gathered by someone else; data that already exists.

(c) **Three good, clear reasons**, so full marks.

(d) Phil gains 4 marks for the first ethical problem identified and described. However, the second point he makes isn't really an ethical one so much as a **practical** one about the **researcher's own self-interest** – that if you get caught, you might suffer for it. Remember, **ethical means 'to do with morality or right and wrong'**. A second point Phil could have made is that the researcher may have to participate in immoral or illegal activities in order **to preserve his or her 'cover'**.

Don't forget...

Read the question **very carefully**! Phil threw away two easy marks on question (a).

An example can help you to explain a term, **but it isn't an explanation in itself**.

(e) Using material from any studies with which you are familiar, explain why it is said that participant observation produces valid but unreliable and unrepresentative data (**Item A**). [20 marks]

PHIL'S ANSWER

Participant observation is often said to produce valid but unreliable and unrepresentative data. It is one of several methods favoured by interactionists to produce qualitative data which gives insight into people's meanings, as Item A says.

There are different types of observation, including non-participant observation, where the observer doesn't try to integrate into the group but just observes. Whereas with participant observation (PO), the sociologist actually joins in with the group's life. There are two kinds of PO, overt and covert PO.

The advantages with PO are that you get a true, i.e. valid picture or feeling of what is happening and why, and you can study in great detail. Also if the group accept the researcher they will act more naturally than if an observer from outside the group was watching. If you are closely involved, e.g. joining in everything they do, you will get a better understanding and more accurate interpretation of their behaviour, as Barker did with the Moonies.

The disadvantages of PO are that it may be difficult to integrate into the group you are studying. If you integrate successfully there is also the danger that you may create bonds with the people you are observing. This may affect your interpretations of what is happening or make you biased in their favour.

An advantage of covert PO is that it allows you to get even closer to the group you want to study, because they don't know your real aims or identity, so they treat you as one of them. This happened to James Patrick when pretending to be a member of a teenage gang in Glasgow. But this can put you in danger if they find out your real identity.

A major problem with PO though is that it takes a long time, so you can't study very many people at a time, and it doesn't produce quantitative data, so it's not very reliable, i.e. it can't be repeated by someone else. Nevertheless, these disadvantages are made up for by the great validity of the data it produces.

10/20

Good start – second sentence takes some relevant points from Item A. But it would be a good idea to define and explain the importance of validity, reliability and representativeness.

First sentence isn't relevant – question isn't about non-PO. Useful distinction between overt and covert, but Phil needs to link it to validity.

Quite good – starts to deal with *why* PO produces validity. Could use Barker example more to illustrate strengths. The interpretivist concept of *verstehen* (subjective understanding) would be useful.

**Useful, but needs to say *how* these things threaten validity, i.e. how they make findings less truthful.

**This is a 'validity' advantage, so Phil should say so.

At last! Phil brings in reliability and hints at representativeness. But these need developing much more and shouldn't be left until the final paragraph.

How to score full marks

- **Define any key technical terms that are used in the question**. Phil didn't do this systematically – he clearly understands **validity** but only gives the briefest of definitions, and then not until paragraph 3 ('true, i.e. valid'); he doesn't define **reliability** until the last paragraph, and he doesn't define **representativeness** at all.

- These terms are central to the question, so as well as just defining them, you need to **explain carefully the importance of each one** – e.g. if the sample is unrepresentative, it won't be possible to generalise the findings to other groups. You must also **link these points to the question** – e.g. because PO studies small groups and because access to them is often a matter of chance, groups studied are unlikely to be representative.

- Aim to **write a balanced answer**. Phil does reasonably well with validity, but needs a lot more on reliability or representativeness.

- **Don't leave key points until the very end**. Phil leaves reliability and representativeness until the final paragraph. If they're important, you need to **raise them in the main body of your answer** – that way, you can explain, illustrate and develop them fully.

- **Use studies** – the question tells you to. Phil mentions two PO studies but gives no real detail of Barker and doesn't link Patrick's study to validity explicitly. Other studies could be used (e.g. **Whyte, Liebow, Ditton, Pryce, Humphreys, etc.**), but you must always link them in properly. Remember to discuss their **methods** and don't get too drawn into describing their findings in a 'Sociological Methods' question.

- Keep it **relevant**. Material is fairly well linked to the question, but a few points go astray – e.g. Phil hasn't really made the references to non-participant observation, or the 'danger' criticism of covert PO, relevant to this question.

Don't forget ...

Use examples from sociological studies to illustrate some of your points. This will show the examiner both **your sociological knowledge** and **your ability to interpret it** to answer the question.

Reliability, validity and representativeness crop up all the time in 'Sociological Methods'. Make sure you know what they mean and how they apply to **all** the different methods and sources of data.

(f) Using material from **Item B** and elsewhere, assess the usefulness of official statistics as a source of data for sociologists.

[20 marks]

PHIL'S ANSWER

As Item B states, official statistics have many advantages. They are readily available because the government publishes them, and cost nothing to use. Because the government collects them, this saves the sociologist time, too. Also as Item B says, 'They are frequently the only available source of data in a particular area', e.g. births. Because they are collected regularly, they also 'allow examination of trends over time', e.g. to see if birth rates are rising. If they are, we can develop a hypothesis and use other stats to test it, like Durkheim did with suicide rates.

Also, they are large-scale (e.g. total UK unemployment), so they are representative of the whole society and we can use them to make generalisations. Sometimes they might be the only source of data on a subject. They can also be useful as background information on a topic before researching it in other ways, e.g. the statistics might show that a particular ethnic group has a very high truancy rate at school. We could then do a small-scale study on a sample of that group to explore why this pattern was happening, maybe using in-depth interviews. (This is triangulation, where two methods are used together.)

As they are collected by professional people, they are also likely to be reliable. Reliability (being able to get the same result when a different researcher repeats the research) is one reason official statistics are favoured by positivists.

On the other hand, interpretivists (interactionists) don't trust official stats. As Item B says, 'They have been collected for a particular purpose, which has influenced how, when and for whom they were collected'. For example, the government might collect figures on unemployment in a particular way so as to make themselves look good, e.g. by keeping the figures low.

Also, if the police decide not to record a crime that you have reported to them, for example, it won't get into the statistics, even though it actually occurred. Also, if they can get a criminal to confess to a lot of crimes that he didn't do, this will improve their clear-up rate and make them look efficient.

So although official statistics have their uses, they suffer from a lot of drawbacks too. In the end, it all depends on what perspective you prefer. Positivists think they are reliable, whereas interpretivists see them as biased.

13/20

Good start: good use of Item and his own example (birth rates) to explain some advantages. 'Durkheim' point is good, but needs developing.

Good point about generalisation – pity Phil didn't explain this in his previous answer, too! 'Truancy' example is good. 'Only source of data' sentence is needless repetition.

Interesting, but too brief! Why is reliability important to positivists? Needs linking up with earlier points about Durkheim, hypotheses and generalisations.

Uses Item, but example isn't well developed. Needs to say how and why government might do this.

Suitable examples, but they need explaining sociologically – e.g. by linking to interpretivist theory and/or concept of validity.

Tries to tie it up, but does it really 'all' depend on perspective? If so, Phil should have outlined this near the start of his answer.

How to score full marks

- **Plan it more carefully**. Phil tells us at the very end that the answer to the question '**all** depends on what perspective you prefer'. If it's really that important, he should have said so **much earlier**. The rest of his answer shows some awareness of different perspectives, but if he had explained clearly what these were earlier on, he could have linked it together more effectively.

- Say more about **critical views**. The **interpretivist** Cicourel distinguishes between '**topic**' and '**resource**'. He says positivists use statistics uncritically as a resource to provide '**social facts**', whereas he claims we should treat them as a topic to be explained – e.g. the crime rate or suicide rate is not a social fact but a **social construction**: the result of interaction processes (as Item B notes) between police/suspects or coroner/witnesses, etc.

- Make the point that official statistics are accused of **lacking validity**. But be sure you know what the term means and how it applies!

- **Marxist** views of official statistics as ruling-class **ideology** could also be brought in – e.g. to provide an explanation for Phil's example about unemployment statistics.

- **Avoid needless repetition** – Phil makes the same point twice about statistics as the only source of data.

- **Avoid sweeping conclusions that your answer won't support**. Phil's conclusion that it's '**all**' about perspectives is also debatable. Theoretical perspectives are important: positivists favour the use of statistics, while interpretivists are more critical. But as he pointed out earlier, there are **other, practical reasons** for using them (they're free, quick, available, etc.) – or for not using them (they might not exist on the subject you're studying).

Don't forget ...

Plan before you write.

Check for repetitions. If possible, avoid by good planning. If necessary, delete after careful proofreading.

Remember that **official statistics** – like other methods and sources – can have both theoretical and practical **advantages** and **disadvantages**.

Methods and sources of data: Sociologists use data from **primary sources** such as structured and unstructured interviews, questionnaires, participant observation and occasionally experiments. They also use **secondary sources** such as official statistics, government reports, diaries, letters and media output.

Perspectives and methods: **Positivists** see sociology as a science. They prefer **quantitative** (numerical) data from questionnaires, structured interviews and official statistics with which to establish social facts and formulate causal laws. **Interpretivists** do not believe humans can be studied in the same way that scientists study nature. Humans give meanings to their actions, and to study these we need to use **qualitative** methods and sources such as unstructured interviews, participant observation and diaries.

Choice of methods: Many factors influence sociologists' choice of method, such as the availability of **resources** (time and money), who funds the research, the nature of the **topic** or group they wish to study, their own **skills** and characteristics, and the theoretical **perspective** from which they study, as well as **ethical** factors such as whether it is right to study people without their consent. These factors also influence a sociologist's choice of topic, as do the sociologist's **personal values** and **previous studies** of the topic.

Strengths and limitations of different sources and methods: All sources of data and methods of research have both strengths and limitations. Each method or source can be evaluated in terms of how **reliable**, **valid** or **representative** are the data that it produces, as well as in terms of **practical concerns** such as time and cost, and **ethical concerns**. Generally, methods that produce valid data (such as participant observation) are less likely to produce reliable data and vice versa.

Item A

Festinger and his colleagues wished to study what happened in a religious sect when their prophecy that the world was coming to an end on a particular day turned out to be wrong (Festinger, Rieken and Schachter 1956). In order to do this they traced, via a newspaper report, a certain Mrs Keech, who had prophesied that a flood would cover the earth's surface from the Arctic Circle to the Gulf of Mexico, but that the faithful would be saved by a flying saucer at midnight on the day of the flood, 21 December. Several researchers joined the group, masquerading as believers, and were thus present when midnight came and went without the prophecy being fulfilled.

Source: from Patrick McNeill, *Research Methods* (Tavistock Publications, 1985)

Item B

The postal questionnaire can be quite a cheap method of gathering data, costing perhaps a third of a similar-sized survey conducted using interviews. Another advantage that a postal questionnaire has over interviews is that respondents have time to think about their answers rather than feeling pressured by the presence of an interviewer into saying the first thing that comes into their head. On the other hand, a postal questionnaire must be designed with the greatest care since there will be no-one there to clarify any misunderstandings that may arise when a respondent comes to answer the questions in it.

(a) Explain why sociologists often use a pilot study when designing a questionnaire. [2 marks]

(b) Suggest **two** differences between structured and unstructured interviews. [4 marks]

(c) Suggest **three** reasons for using questionnaires in sociological research other than those mentioned in **Item B**. [6 marks]

(d) Identify and briefly explain **two** problems that Festinger and his colleagues might have faced in conducting their research (**Item A**). [8 marks]

(e) Explain why unstructured interviews and participant observation may be more useful methods of research than written questionnaires. [20 marks]

(f) Using material from **the Items** and elsewhere, assess the relative importance of practical, theoretical and ethical issues in choosing an appropriate research method. [20 marks]

Examiner's hints

- In (e), remember to stick to the advantages of PO and unstructured interviews over written questionnaires – don't be tempted to start giving all the advantages and disadvantages of each one, or it will take all day! Link your discussion to 'positivism versus interpretivism', and use studies that have employed these three methods.

- In (f), you must say something about all three issues. Practical issues include time, cost, preferences of the research's funders, etc. Theoretical issues can be linked to positivist and interpretivist preferences for quantitative and qualitative data, respectively. Ethics is about moral issues – some methods involve deceiving subjects. Again, use studies to illustrate points wherever possible.

Answers can be found on pages 94–96.

Answers to Questions to try

1 Families and Households

How to score full marks

(a) Ten.

> **Examiner's comment**
> Correct answer: 38 minus 28 = 10.

(b) 1. It is usually thought of as having a male full-time breadwinner (Parsons' instrumental role), while the wife is a full-time housewife (Parsons' expressive role).

2. It is usually thought of as middle class (or at least affluent upper working class) and white.

> **Examiner's comment**
> More than two features are given here, and all of them are acceptable.

(c) 1. Childcare policies will affect whether mothers can go out to work.

2. Easier divorce laws will affect whether couples stay together.

3. Government benefit policies may make it not worthwhile for married women to claim social security when unemployed, thus reinforcing dependence on their husbands.

> **Examiner's comment**
> All three policies given are suitable, as are many others like taxation policies, education policies, etc.

(d) 1. Capitalism requires that its labour force be serviced and its needs met if possible at no cost to the employer. Thus women are encouraged to take on the housewife role in which they 'reproduce' their husbands' labour power for free, cooking meals, doing housework, providing sexual services, etc.

2. The capitalist economy needs docile workers who will accept the authority of their bosses. In the family, children are socialised into obedience to authority, thus preparing them for a future role as exploited and subordinate workers.

> **Examiner's comment**
> This answer identifies and clearly describes two appropriate ways. Both come from a Marxist perspective – the one most closely associated with the idea that the family serves the interests of capitalism.

(e) Sociologists use the term 'social construction' to show that people's roles aren't 'natural'. Social construction means created by society, i.e. society has shaped or defined a role to be the way it is. Because societies differ from place to place (or over time, e.g. Britain in pre-industrial times versus today), they construct roles and statuses differently.

For example, people often think the housewife role is 'natural', maybe because women are thought to have a maternal or nurturing instinct. If this was true, though, we ought to find all women in all societies adopting this role. But in Israel women serve in the army (a non-nurturing role!) and in some tribal societies studied by Mead, women took a 'masculine' role while the men performed the domestic tasks. Ann Oakley argues that today's housewife role evolved only in the nineteenth century, with industrialisation. Before then, all family members worked together in cottage industries. After the industrial revolution, however, women were pushed out of paid work and back into the home, e.g. by the Factory Acts banning them from working in coalmines, making them dependent on their husbands and thus much more vulnerable.

Children too were pushed out of the factories by laws banning child labour, and compulsory schooling after 1870 also prevented them working. They came to be seen as innocent and vulnerable, in need of protection from the corruption and danger of the adult world. Ariès argues that this process began about the sixteenth or seventeenth century. Before that, children were seen as miniature adults and very early began to play a part in society (e.g. from about age 7 they would be working). Postman argues that the rise of adult literacy created childhood as a separate status – once adults could read and write, they could have secrets children couldn't gain access to (e.g. about sex, death, etc.).

Nowadays, Postman argues, childhood is disappearing – e.g. television shows sex, violence, etc. and adults no longer have special knowledge. Also, the idea of children's rights is redefining their status.

Therefore as we have seen, both the housewife role and childhood can be seen as socially constructed, because society has shaped them differently at different times. Some would even say that they are both a modern western invention.

Examiner's comment

This is a very thorough answer which explains clearly the meaning of the idea of social construction and goes on to apply this to **both aspects** of the question – the housewife role and childhood. The answer outlines relevant arguments, such as the idea that if the housewife role were not socially constructed, then we should expect to find all women adopting the same role everywhere. It goes on to use **appropriate evidence** from a range of different sources to show historical and cross-cultural variations in the way the position of children and women is defined. It would have been interesting if we had been told a little more about how children's rights are redefining children's status. The main points are drawn together well and an appropriate **conclusion** links back to the set question.

(f) Some sociologists argue that in modern society there is only one dominant form, namely the nuclear family. Functionalists like Parsons argue that it uniquely fits the needs of modern industrial society, enabling mobility to occur. To some extent, Marxists and feminists also assume that the 'conventional' family type described in Item B (i.e. sexual division of labour, dominant breadwinning male) is dominant – because it serves the needs of capitalism or patriarchy.

However, as Item B also shows, this family type is becoming less common. More women are going out to work and, according to Hilary Land, in 1 in 5 households the woman is the main earner. More women now remain unmarried and/or childless. Divorce is increasing the number of remarriages and step-families. All this is producing more diversity in family forms. However, Chester argues that we now have a 'neo-conventional' family which is the same as the conventional family but for married women going out to work. Most children still grow up in two-parent families.

As Item B shows, there are different kinds of diversity. For example, different ethnic groups have their own family patterns – e.g. extended families are more common among Asians and Cypriots. Similarly, family structures change with the life cycle – e.g. newly weds, young children, empty nest couples, widowed. The Rapoports argue that we have moved from a single 'normative' conventional nuclear family form to a 'pluralistic' set-up where a range of different forms is accepted. This might explain the decline in stigma attached to forms such as lone parents, 'illegitimate' children, divorce, gay households, etc. However, functionalists and New Right thinkers argue that such forms are deviant and dysfunctional. For them, a heterosexual nuclear family with a clear sexual division of labour is essential.

Some sociologists believe we are now in a late modern or postmodern period, and this may explain increased diversity. Giddens argues that family forms have become more fluid and it is better now to speak of coupling and de-coupling as the key feature. Likewise, Stacey's study of the 'divorce extended family' argues that we have now reached the point where we can no longer talk about 'the' family – family life is now so fluid and diverse. This is like Morgan's idea of 'family practices' – we need to look at the diversity of what people think of as 'family' and stop trying to classify into types altogether.

Thus there is a range of conflicting contributions, from the functionalist view that there is only one 'normal' family form (and that other forms are deviant) to the idea that diversity is growing and we can no longer speak of 'the' family as a single fixed entity. However, there seems no doubt that diversity is on the increase.

Examiner's comment
This answer **uses the Item** (as instructed to do so by the question) very effectively to illustrate the idea of the conventional family and the types and extent of diversity. It outlines **a range of contributions,** such as functionalist, Marxist, feminist, pluralist, New Right and postmodernist. It **evaluates** the contribution of some of these approaches in terms of how far they help us to understand particular **trends** or are backed up by **evidence.** Finally, there is a brief but relevant **conclusion.**

🎯 How to score full marks

(a) A label is a definition attached to someone saying what they are or what their status is, e.g. that someone is 'insane'. This may lead to people treating that person in a different way.

> **Examiner's comment**
> Very good explanation. A psychiatrist's diagnosis of a patient as 'schizophrenic' is a form of labelling.

(b) The first difference between working-class and middle-class life-styles which may affect health chances, is smoking. Manual workers are more likely than non-manual workers to smoke cigarettes.

A second difference could be alcohol consumption. Manual workers drink more than non-manual.

> **Examiner's comment**
> Good. Doesn't fall into the trap of giving an example from the Item (such as diet or exercise), since the question forbids this. Other possible answers could include greater up-take of health care services (such as vaccinations, dental check-ups and ante-natal services) by the middle class.

(c) 1. If you are labelled schizophrenic, you may be locked up in a mental hospital against your will.

2. When you come out of hospital, even if you have recovered, others may see you as 'mad' or 'unstable' and so you might find it hard to get a job (like 'ex-cons').

3. Some people labelled and treated as schizophrenic (e.g. put in mental hospital, made to take drugs etc.) can become mentally ill or even suicidal as a result of this treatment.

> **Examiner's comment**
> Three appropriate ways suggested. All of them show how, once a person is labelled, negative consequences may follow. Other possible adverse effects can include homelessness upon discharge from hospital, loss of social networks through being hospitalised, family break-up etc.

(d) 1. One criticism is that people can be mentally ill because of all sorts of reasons and social factors. For example, if you lose a loved one (e.g. through death or divorce), this may make you mentally disturbed. All the psychiatrist is doing by labelling you is confirming that you have a problem – he/she isn't the cause of the problem.

2. You can also be mentally ill without ever going near a psychiatrist to get labelled. For example, some cultures don't have psychiatrists but do have mental illness, so logically mental illness couldn't (in those societies) be caused by psychiatric labelling.

> **Examiner's comment**
> Two very good criticisms, well described. Another possible criticism might be that psychiatrists alone may not create the label – relatives, friends, social workers, GPs, even the patients themselves may all play a part in creating the label. For example, much mental illness is dealt with by GPs, not psychiatrists.

(e) Compared with the past, we are now healthier and live longer lives. For example, average life expectancy in 1900 was under 50 (partly because of high infant mortality of about 150 per 1000). Why have things improved? We often read about the latest wonder drug and most people probably think of scientific medicine and doctors as the main reason why our health is better today.

However, sociologists (and social historians) criticise this commonsense view of the role of medicine. For example, McKeown studied the First World War, when many doctors were serving abroad in the army and many hospitals were being used for wounded soldiers. Yet he found that death rates for the civilian population actually fell. This was because of social and economic factors like full employment (there was lots of work available in the war industries).

Similarly, in the Second World War, which followed the 'great depression' period of unemployment, there was rationing of basic foodstuffs which meant that the poor actually got a better diet than they could have afforded otherwise. This improved their health rather than anything the doctors could do. Wilkinson also argues that the sense of national solidarity was good for people's sense of well-being, so this may have been good for mental health too.

Another way we can see what effect medicine has is by looking at tuberculosis (TB). In the 19th century, TB was a leading cause of death. Yet by the 1940s, it had already fallen to a few thousand deaths per year. Yet this was before a real cure (antibiotics) was widely available, and before there was a vaccine to prevent it. Hart argues that the decline was due not to the medical profession but to improvements in living conditions, such as better housing and diets, etc., and less poverty (TB is particularly linked to poverty – one of the main groups to suffer from it today in Britain is the homeless).

A lot of other disease is linked to poor social conditions. In the Industrial Revolution, many people died from infectious diseases such as typhoid, typhus, cholera etc. But as social conditions improved, e.g. with clean drinking water and proper sewers, these diseases killed fewer people. Also living standards improved so people had better diets and built up their immune systems against disease.

Also today, the main killers are cancer and heart disease, which medicine hasn't been very successful against. But we know that factors like diet, smoking and alcohol all play an important part in these diseases. If we wanted to cut death rates, we would have more success if we could stop people smoking, rather than spending millions on high-tech transplants or wonder drugs. However, it can also be argued in defence of modern medicine that it is now much more effective than in the past. For example, new discoveries in genetics may bring rapid medical advances. As yet, though, this has not really happened and although medicine and doctors can sometimes cure individuals, social and political changes can prevent diseases hitting whole populations.

Examiner's comment
This answer shows a **good knowledge and understanding** of relevant material and **applies it well** to the question. A good opening paragraph shows awareness of just how much health has improved and hints that the commonsense view of the role of medicine and the medical profession might be wrong. Then it gives an account of a range of material on the **relative importance of social, as against medical, factors** in explaining why health has improved. The concluding paragraph suggests that medicine may be able to make some contribution, but reaches a reasoned conclusion that social changes are more important.

(f) As the Black Report demonstrated, middle-class people are healthier and live longer than the working class – death rates for unskilled men of working age are about 2.5 times higher than for professionals. One sociological explanation for these inequalities, described in Item B, is that they are due to behavioural differences between classes.

Item B describes class differences in behaviour, such as that poorer people eat worse diets. Middle-class people also take more exercise and smoke less – e.g. 45% of unskilled manual men smoke, but only 15% of professional men. These differences cause health differences – smoking causes lung disease, the wrong diet causes heart disease etc.

Some sociologists' explanations go further. As Item B says, they see class differences in behaviour as the result of subcultural differences. For example, some functionalists argue that the lower working class place value on immediate gratification, toughness etc. This could then explain why unskilled men drink more (to be 'a real man'), smoke more (live for today without thought for their future health) etc. One former Conservative health minister said that working-class northerners had worse health because their culture valued fish and chips, beer and cigarettes rather than healthier lifestyles. On this basis, the solution might be to change working-class culture and behaviour by health education campaigns aimed at persuading them to quit smoking etc.

However, although behaviour does affect health, and sometimes culture affects behaviour, other factors may also be at work. The most important alternative explanation is the materialist or structural one. This says that it is material factors like income, job security/unemployment, working conditions, housing etc. that determine class differences in health. Working-class people are poorer, have less control over their jobs and their lives in general, are more at risk of unemployment, live in worse housing etc. and all this damages their health. For example, Brenner shows how unemployment (more a threat for manual workers) is linked to suicide, cancer and heart disease.

Other research also shows that behaviour may only be part of the explanation. The Alameda County longitudinal study in California controlled for a range of risk behaviour (smoking, exercise, diet etc.), yet still found that the lowest income group had three times the death rate from heart disease of the top income group. This suggests that other factors, such as material ones, may play a greater part than culture or behaviour.

Even if behaviour does affect health, behaviour may be a response to structural factors rather than cultural ones. Hilary Graham argues that working-class women know that smoking is bad for their health, but continue to smoke because it enables them to cope with the stresses of managing their family's welfare with few resources.

Overall, then, behaviour differs between classes and this probably has some effect on health differences, although as the Alameda County study shows, behaviour may have only limited effects on health. And as Graham argues, material factors may be more important than cultural factors in shaping behaviour and causing illness.

Examiner's comment
A **well-argued** answer to the question. It outlines **relevant evidence**, from Item B and elsewhere, of class differences in health and in behaviour and examines behavioural and cultural **explanations** of health inequalities. These are then **effectively evaluated** from the standpoint of the materialist/structural explanation, drawing on evidence from appropriate studies before arriving at a **reasoned conclusion** as to the view in the question.

🎯 How to score full marks

(a) Content analysis is a method of studying the media where the researcher identifies a set of categories (e.g. particular types of gender role) and then counts how often each one appears in the media (or in a particular kind of output, e.g. a soap series).

> **Examiner's comment**
> A clear explanation that earns both the marks.

(b) One criticism of the use of content analysis is that simply counting the number of times something turns up tells us nothing about the meaning of that thing, because it is taken out of its context.

A second criticism is that it can be difficult to decide what is the right category into which to put a particular case.

We could also add another problem – that the categories are chosen arbitrarily by the researcher, i.e. it just imposes the researcher's view of what is important.

> **Examiner's comment**
> All three of these criticisms are correct and relevant. There is no harm in adding another point – so long as you get two of them right, you get the marks.

(c) Three useful concepts would be: agenda-setting, news values, hierarchies of credibility. Another would be manufacture of news.

> **Examiner's comment**
> All correct. Note that you don't need to do more than name them.

(d) One reason is that audiences are not just passive recipients of media messages. Many approaches stress that individuals can resist the output of the media, for example because they have an alternative or oppositional value system that rejects the ideology put forward by the media.

Another reason is that the influence of the media is more likely to be indirect than direct. The real influence of the media is in its long-term messages, for example constantly showing women in subordinate positions seeps into people's consciousness.

> **Examiner's comment**
> Two good reasons, clearly explained. The hypodermic syringe model is the one most closely associated with the idea of a direct (and immediate) influence on audiences, but other approaches, such as the two-step flow and hegemonic models, reject this. Other sociologists would also say that the media merely reflect the attitudes and values of their audiences anyway, so cannot exercise much influence over them.

(e) The media are a powerful source of information, transmitting images and ideas to the population – including images and ideas about ethnicity and ethnic groups. Many have accused the media of representing minority groups in terms of stereotypes, treating all members of a group as if they were the same. As Item A says, minorities, especially black ones, have often been represented as a threat.

Hartmann and Husband found that press coverage of 'race' issues was presented in terms of threats and conflicts. For example, immigration was a major focus of press coverage and much space was given to the views of politicians opposed to immigration, who argued that it would lead to conflict and would 'swamp' British culture. Much more space was given to immigrants as a problem than to the problems faced by immigrants. Although their study was carried out in the 1970s, it holds good today, with recent coverage of immigration in similar negative terms – 'bogus asylum seekers' and 'economic migrants' 'flooding' into Britain to take advantage of the supposed generosity of the welfare state. According to Hartmann and Husband, the media set the framework of interpretation for the public to think about 'race' issues.

Stuart Hall's Marxist approach in 'Policing the Crisis' looked at how black youth came to be portrayed by the media as violent muggers in the 1970s and (like Hartmann and Husband) a threat to law and order. The media created a moral panic about this supposed threat, which was then used to divide black and white workers and help secure the rule of the bourgeoisie by justifying a more repressive state.

The media are often our only source of information about foreign countries. Television, for example, brings us images of people in Third World countries which create a framework of interpretation through which we understand the world. These images present us with a view of people in Africa as incapable of ruling or even feeding themselves and as savages engaged in irrational, murderous tribal conflicts. Many of these ideas can be traced back to Britain's colonial past, when racist ideas were used to justify white domination, but they live on in media images even after Britain's empire has gone. Also, because the media focus on the immediate, they rarely explain the historical roots of Africa's present problems and conflicts.

This is like Alvarado's view that we can understand media representation of black people in terms of four categories – the exotic, the dangerous, the humorous, the pitied. For example, the coverage of famines is an example of 'the pitied'. Pictures of starving black people tell us they are to be pitied, but also that they are inferior and dependent on 'us', the west, for survival. Stuart Hall makes a similar point with the idea of the 'white eye' – i.e. the media look at blacks from a white standpoint. This is an example of institutional racism in the media.

However, not all media representations of ethnicity are the same. There is a significant ethnic minority press (e.g. 'The Voice' newspaper), minority programming on television, etc. While non-white actors are often typecast in stereotyped roles or marginalised, as Item A suggests, there are also some signs of change. In America, non-whites are getting more parts in mainstream television and are represented in more 'normal' roles.

Finally, we can note the effect that some of these representations have on the majority population. Van Dijk studied press headlines after the inner city disturbances of 1985, which contained words like race, riot, violence, black, police, etc. Two years on, he interviewed people and found they could recall the events and that they described them using this kind of language as their framework of interpretation, rather than ideas of neo-colonialism, racism, etc. This suggests both that the media represent ethnicity in particular ways and that this shapes the way people think about the subject.

> **Examiner's comment**
> A good, solid account of a number of ways in which ethnicity is represented in the media. Clear explanations of several sociological **studies** are linked by **concepts** such as frameworks of interpretation and put into some theoretical context by using Hall's Marxist approach. The answer also shows awareness of **different types of media and representation**, such as the black press in Britain and news, sitcoms, etc. A useful last paragraph shows the importance of these representations in shaping how people think about race and ethnicity.

(f) Ideology is a term associated with Marxism. Miliband's Marxist instrumentalism argues that the media are the direct tool of the ruling class for spreading pro-capitalist ideology, as Item B shows – a means of ideological control, indoctrinating the population with conservative ideas and discrediting radical alternative views, making sure its ideas are the ruling ones, as Item B says.

In this view capitalists own and control the media – only the rich can afford to. (Murdock and Golding point to growing concentration of ownership.) Journalists and editors are their servants. Media output is all very similar, reflecting the same ruling-class perspective on events, so the audience has little choice over the news they receive, constantly reinforcing the ideology. Pluralists criticise this view, arguing that while owners may have allocative control (over resources) they don't have operational control (over day-to-day output). However, owners can always fire editors who don't produce the 'right' output.

Marcuse extends these ideas, arguing that media output creates a 'one-dimensional' reality where opposition to capitalism becomes impossible. The media distract the proletariat from their exploitation with trivia (soaps, game shows), producing false consciousness. However, Marcuse's views have been criticised as elitist since they are about the impossibility of change, rather than class society and overthrow of capitalism.

Althusser argues that the media is an 'ideological state apparatus' (ISA). Unlike the repressive state apparatus which maintains power through coercion, ISAs win acceptance of capitalist rule. As Item B puts it, 'The ruling class is thus able to rule through ideas rather than through using force'. The media do this by producing an 'imaginary' picture of the world which conceals the reality of exploitation. But unlike the instrumentalist view, Althusser argues that to do this they must be relatively autonomous from the ruling class – otherwise they would appear biased and be disbelieved, serving no function for the ruling class.

Gramsci uses a similar concept, 'hegemony' – rule by consent rather than force. The media do this by creating a 'common sense' (i.e. ideology), e.g. that inequality is inevitable (between classes, races, etc.), our leaders know best, etc. Stuart Hall has used Gramsci's ideas to explain the moral panic about mugging in the 1970s. British capitalism was going into a crisis and needed public consent for stronger state powers and so represented this as a problem of law and order. The media gave access to authority figures (politicians, police, etc.) as 'primary definers' of the crisis, helping to legitimate a tougher stance and used mugging as a justification for strengthening the state for tougher action against disorder.

Another Marxist-oriented study of media output as ideology is the Glasgow Media Group. They looked at the media's focus on strikes. They found the media produced stories structured around the ideas that strikes are always bad, that management is rational and workers irrational, that workers' wage claims were the cause of inflation. All this supports capitalism by turning the public against the strikers.

However, not all output favours the ruling class. Pluralists argue that we choose what to read/watch and alternative views can be found in minority publications. The fact that most people choose to watch/read the same kinds of thing simply means there is a consensus. Marxists reply that the consensus is engineered by the powerful. Even if minority views do sometimes get expressed, the *dominant* ideology is still pro-capitalist.

Feminists claim that the media also produce patriarchal, not just capitalist, ideology, justifying female subordination. For example, McRobbie argues that magazines like 'Jackie' encourage girls to be passive, preoccupied with finding a man, etc. Others criticise the claim that media output is inevitably ideological, arguing that there is no clear method for deciding what is and isn't 'ideological' – it all depends on your interpretation of the media message. And since messages are polysemic (many meanings) depending on who receives them, what for a Marxist is ideology might not be for someone else. Finally, postmodernists argue that 'ideology' assumes we can get at an underlying reality that the ideology conceals, whereas (they claim) there is nothing underlying it. All there is are the surface media images – they are the reality.

Examiner's comment
This is a very thorough answer indeed. It recognises the Marxist origins of the notion of 'ideology' and goes on to **describe and evaluate a range of different Marxist theories and studies.** It draws on material from the Item (as instructed to do so by the question) and uses **other approaches** – including pluralism, feminism and postmodernism – **to evaluate** the view.

How to score full marks

(a) 'Streaming' is the process of grouping pupils into separate classes on the basis of differences in ability. For example, those pupils seen as cleverest will all be put together into the 'A' stream and will stay together for all their subjects.

> **Examiner's comment**
> A very full, clear answer

(b) One example of a way in which the school curriculum can be seen as ethnocentric is that it may focus on British history as opposed to the history of e.g. India or Africa.

Another example is that the focus of RE is mainly on Christianity rather than religions of other non-white pupils such as Hinduism or the Sikh religion.

> **Examiner's comment**
> Both these are good examples. You could also give examples from geography, literature etc.

(c) The first way that schools act as agencies of socialisation is by teaching skills needed in later life for earning a living.

Secondly, they teach children to work together and cooperate with other individuals, even if they don't know or like them.

Thirdly, they socialise pupils into society's values.

> **Examiner's comment**
> These are all correct answers.

(d) 1. In recent years, there have been changes in women's roles in society, especially at work, and this has had a knock-on effect on girls' educational achievement. Girls now have more job opportunities and higher aspirations, so they see the value of good GCSEs and are prepared to work harder at school to achieve them, thus overtaking the boys.

2. In schools, there is now more awareness of equality of opportunity between the sexes and more effort to give girls an equal (or more than equal) chance, e.g. teachers being trained to ensure girls get equal attention or use of facilities. This results in better performance at GCSE and beyond.

> **Examiner's comment**
> Two reasons – changes at work and in school – identified and clearly explained. Other reasons could include more female role models, or changes in females' domestic roles or their expectations about marriage.

(e) Research shows that working-class pupils generally do worse than higher-class pupils, and some explanations have focused on factors outside the school like home background. However, interactionists argue that we should look instead at processes within schools, since it is interactions between pupils and teachers that construct success and failure.

Many studies in different schools show this. Rist studied a kindergarten and showed how the teacher had grouped children within a few days onto different tables. The ones she thought were brightest (the Tigers) were mainly middle class, whereas the ones she thought were least interested (the Clowns) were working class. Sharp and Green's study of a primary school found that teachers saw the working-class kids as not yet 'ready' to learn to read, so ended up giving their attention to the middle-class kids. These studies are both examples of labelling, where teachers have expectations about children's abilities/characters based on stereotypes.

These labels are often used to treat children differently, and since according to Becker teachers operate with a stereotype of the 'ideal pupil' as basically middle class, these children get treated more favourably. One result is the self-fulfilling prophecy, where the child actually becomes what the teacher labelled him/her as. Rosenthal and Jacobson did a study where they told teachers that a proportion of the pupils (who the researchers had actually selected at random) would spurt ahead in the coming year. On returning, they found that about half of these randomly chosen children had spurted ahead – simply because their teachers believed that they would and so treated them differently.

Streaming can also become a self-fulfilling prophecy. Ball calls this differentiation – the school differentiates between pupils on the basis (supposedly) of ability, though this usually leads to working-class pupils ending up in lower streams. Teachers take a different attitude to different streams, even offering them a different curriculum, as Keddie showed. Pupils in lower streams 'get the message' that they are not as valued by school and may turn to anti-school subcultures as an alternative source of status. Since these reject the school's values, e.g. 'having a laff' (Willis) and truanting, they are likely to lead to failure.

The hidden curriculum is related to these processes. It is all those things that are not officially taught but are absorbed by the pupils. For example, Hargreaves argues that schools give off the message that it is bad to be working class. Schools have a middle-class 'ethos' or values/atmosphere, so if you are working class you may feel you don't fit in. Bourdieu, a Marxist, argues that this leads to the self-elimination of working-class pupils, who drop out. He also argues that the school teaches the cultural capital of the middle classes, things they value like classical music or art for art's sake, which working-class pupils are alienated from and so tend to fail in.

However, these processes don't inevitably lead to failure. Working-class pupils may reject negative labels, and not all teachers may apply them. In any case, interactionists don't tell us why teachers hold such stereotypes in the first place. To find this out, we would need to look at wider society outside the school.

> **Examiner's comment**
> A **strong knowledge** of a very good range of studies and concepts. Several studies are described accurately, **using key terms** like stereotypes, ideal pupil, labelling, streaming, differentiation, the self-fulfilling prophecy, anti-school subcultures, cultural capital, ethos and so on. The studies are mainly from an **interactionist** perspective, but the answer also shows awareness that **Marxists** like Bourdieu or Willis have something to contribute to understanding the hidden curriculum and processes within schools – both of which are dealt with here. All the material is **well focused** on the question, it starts and finishes well and the conclusion has some brief, but very appropriate, evaluation of the interactionist approach.

(f) Functionalists believe that education performs very important roles for individuals, the economy and the wider social structure, as Item A notes. It provides secondary socialisation, passing on shared culture, enables individuals to develop their potential and regulates their behaviour. Durkheim believed that education created solidarity, uniting individuals and making them realise that they are part of something bigger. An example of this is American schools where pupils sing the national anthem and pledge allegiance to the flag every day, making them feel part of American society.

According to functionalists, school is society in miniature, where pupils have to get on with strangers, and where they learn that status is to be achieved not ascribed as in the family. Parsons argues that schools are the bridge between family and wider society, where children stop being judged by the particularistic norms of their families and are judged instead by universalistic norms of society.

Davis and Moore argue that education plays a selection/allocation function, selecting individuals for the roles that their abilities best suit them for and slotting the most talented into the functionally most important jobs in society, differentiating between pupils, as Item A says, on the basis of their ability. Education does this by offering everyone an equal opportunity to achieve, i.e. it's a meritocracy.

However, Marxists such as Bowles and Gintis criticise the view that education is a meritocracy where children achieve according to their abilities, since children of similar abilities perform differently, with higher-class children doing better. Really, functionalists are just repeating a 'myth' of meritocracy. So long as pupils believe it, it ensures they will accept their place in the class system. Marxists also reject the functionalist claim that education reproduces shared values and norms. They argue that in reality it reproduces the values and norms of the capitalist class, legitimising their power.

The functionalists' view that education provides pupils with the skills for work has also been criticised, since these are often not acquired at school but from additional training by employers. New Right thinkers, and some Labour politicians, criticise schools for teaching things not relevant for work. Others argue that education really only has a baby-sitting or social control function. It's a way of controlling young people and of allowing parents to go out to work.

Functionalists are useful in drawing attention to the many functions education can perform, but they are probably wrong to see them as all being for the good of individuals and society as a whole. For example, it may be only the ruling class who benefit from education producing a docile workforce. From another perspective, interactionists would argue that they have an over-socialised view of individuals and that we can't see education in terms of 'functions' anyway – we should look instead at how individuals interact within schools rather than seeing education as a 'thing' which shapes the individual in society's interests.

Examiner's comment
This answer shows a **sound knowledge** of a range of relevant material of the functionalist and other sociological approaches to education and offers some clear evaluation of the functionalist contribution. It identifies and explains a **number of functions** that functionalists see education as performing, such as socialisation into society's value consensus, its (apparently) meritocratic character and its selection and allocation role, preparing people for work. These functionalist ideas are then criticised effectively by presenting **Marxist** and **New Right** views. Finally, a useful concluding paragraph sums up the argument and introduces a new dimension of evaluation very neatly, by bringing in the **interactionist** view that the whole idea of functional analysis of education (or anything else for that matter) is misplaced.

🎯 How to score full marks

(a) What this means is that more and more of the poor are women, or that women's poverty is becoming more apparent e.g. because feminist sociologists have revealed it to us.

> **Examiner's comment**
> Good answer. Feminists argue that in a patriarchal or male-dominated society, women's poverty is often hidden from view, and that women are more likely to be poor than men.

(b) 1. The poor help to keep social workers in jobs – because poverty causes family stresses etc. and so social workers are needed.

2. Another way poverty benefits the non-poor is that the poor can be made to work for low wages, so employers (part of the non-poor) can exploit them profitably.

> **Examiner's comment**
> Two correct points. You could also say the poor can be pressed into doing the unpleasant jobs no-one else wants, or that they can make the non-poor feel smug and superior.

(c) **(i)** The state provides welfare through, for example, the NHS, which is paid for by public money (taxes etc.).
(ii) Voluntary organisations like Dr Barnardo's provide welfare for families and children.
(iii) The private sector is profit-making businesses, e.g. private nursing homes provide welfare for the sick (as long as they can afford the fees).

> **Examiner's comment**
> Three clear ways in which each sector can provide welfare.

(d) Firstly, most women marry and have children, and they are expected to take the main responsibility for childcare, especially while the children are very young. So they may give up work, at least temporarily, and this means they lose out on pension contributions and rights (especially pensions provided by the employer). So when they retire they get a smaller pension than a man would.

Secondly, even when they are working full-time, women don't usually earn as much as men and so they are likely to have smaller savings than men and so be poor in their old age.

> **Examiner's comment**
> Both points are correct and both are clearly explained.

(e) There have been numerous attempts to measure poverty and there has been disagreement about how to measure it and how much poverty there is. One reason for this is that sociologists don't agree on how to define poverty in the first place. Obviously, if sociologists disagree about definitions, they will measure it differently too.

The main division is between those who prefer an absolute definition and those who say poverty is relative. Those who define it in absolute terms, as a lack of the essentials for physical survival or efficiency, such as Rowntree's classic study, go on to draw up a list of essential nutrients, clothing, etc. and to price this so as to work out a minimum income needed to keep a person out of poverty. They then measure what proportion of the population falls below this income. For example, Rowntree in 1899 found a third of the population were in poverty.

Rowntree also distinguished between primary poverty (insufficient income to meet basic needs) and secondary poverty (where the person theoretically has enough but spends it unwisely and cannot meet their basic needs). One problem here is that it relies on experts (e.g. nutritionists) to say what the essentials are, and the poor are unlikely to have this knowledge so Rowntree's distinction between primary and secondary poverty is rather unrealistic.

Rowntree's way of measuring poverty influenced the welfare state when it was set up in the 1940s, and it still uses an absolute (subsistence) approach for the key means-tested benefit, Income Support. Using this measure, currently about a quarter of the population (and a third of all children) can be defined as poor.

The alternative approach is to see poverty as relative – as an aspect of inequality. It compares the poor with the average of society. On this definition, you are poor if you fall a long way below the average (even if you have plenty to eat, all basic physical needs met, etc.) – e.g. if you live on less than half average income. Townsend (1979) set out to measure poverty using a relative definition. He constructed a 'deprivation index' – a list of items such as a damp-free home, cooked breakfast, etc. He found that once income fell to about 150% of benefit levels, deprivation (measured by how many items you lacked from his list) began to rise sharply. His figures for the 1970s showed a much higher rate of poverty (about 25%) than official figures using an absolute measure (under 6%).

Townsend was criticised for claiming to be objective (scientific) when really he was being subjective – imposing his personal values in trying to measure poverty. For instance, some people don't like cooked breakfasts – does this make them poor! Mack and Lansley partly overcame this with their 'democratic' approach, asking the public what they thought were the essential items instead. This is better, but they still gave them a list from which to choose instead of letting the public draw up their own list from scratch, so this is still subjective. Again, like Townsend, they arrived at a much higher figure for poverty than absolute or official measures.

One problem with measuring relative poverty is that it's not a fixed thing. Because social standards of what is an acceptable standard of living change, you can't easily compare different times, because you are measuring different things – e.g. today you need enough for a TV, phone, fridge, etc. to stay out of relative poverty, but 100 years ago even the rich didn't have these things.

> **Examiner's comment**
> A good answer. It shows how measuring poverty requires the researcher to define it first, and how the definition then affects how much poverty the researcher's measurements find. It examines some of the main studies that have attempted to measure poverty based on these different definitions. It also makes some good evaluative points, such as the criticisms of the distinction between primary and secondary poverty, and in the final paragraph, of measures based on relative definitions.

(f) Individualistic theories see poverty as the result of particular characteristics of poor individuals. For example, in the 19th century it was believed (especially by the middle class) that the poor were largely to blame for their plight because of their irresponsible behaviour, e.g. squandering their wages on drink, not saving for a rainy day, not working hard enough or looking for work when unemployed. The Victorians built workhouses into which the poor had to go if they wanted state support. These were basically prisons for the poor to deter the poor from relying on the state.

The individualistic view was also held by Margaret Thatcher's government in the 1980s, when one of her ministers argued that the unemployed should get on their bikes and look for work, i.e. the solution was in their own hands (or feet!) not the government's.

However, this individualistic view can be criticised on numerous grounds. First of all, as the Victorians found, punishing the poor to discourage them from being 'irresponsible' or 'scroungers' doesn't get rid of poverty (although it might stop some of them seeking state help) – simply because they may be poor through no fault of their own, e.g. through economic depression, when there are no jobs to be had.

Related to this is the criticism that it is an ideology. An ideology is a set of beliefs that covertly justify something, such as the existence of inequality. According to Marxists, the individualistic view of poverty is an ideology which shifts the blame and the attention away from the capitalist class whose exploitation of the workers is the real cause of poverty. Instead, it neatly blames the victims of this exploitation for their misery.

Golding and Middleton did a study of the media and public attitudes to welfare claimants. They argue that 'scroungermania' – media scaremongering and exaggerated stories about benefit cheats and 'scroungers' in the 1970s and 1980s – is an example of an individualistic explanation, because it says that many of the poor are immoral individuals, crooks trying to cheat the taxpayers. They argue that it is an ideology serving ruling-class interests, since (a) it encourages divisions in the working class (e.g. between employed and unemployed) – 'divide and rule' – and (b) it justifies cutting welfare benefits (since they are going to people who don't deserve them), so paying for tax cuts for the rich.

Sociologists regard individualistic explanations as unsociological and prefer explanations which focus on social factors. One such is the Marxist view above, that says that poverty is the product of the structure of capitalist society, and that any member of the working class is at least potentially a member of the poor, e.g. by losing one's job.

However, other sociologists argue that poverty can be due to the subculture of the poor – they are seen as having the wrong attitudes, norms, values, etc. to avoid poverty. Although individuals might be 'irresponsible', etc., as the individualistic view claims, this is because they are doing what their subculture dictates. For example, Oscar Lewis sees the poor as unable to escape poverty because their culture makes them value immediate gratification rather than the deferred gratification needed to succeed at school and get a good job.

Examiner's comment

A very **thorough and well-focused** answer. Individualistic views of the causes of poverty are explained clearly and fully, including 19th-century laissez-faire views and 20th-century Thatcherite views. These approaches are very effectively **evaluated**, mainly from a **Marxist** viewpoint using Golding and Middleton and the concept of ideology, but **Lewis**' culture of poverty approach is also brought in and applied appropriately to the question.

How to score full marks

(a) Automated production is where the whole production process is carried out and even controlled automatically by machines, not by human beings. For example, computers can monitor/regulate the machines that make the product.

> **Examiner's comment**
> A clear, accurate explanation.

(b) One factor that may influence the chance of being unemployed is their qualifications – people without qualifications find it harder to get work.

Another factor is the state of the economy, e.g. if there is a recession or depression, everyone will find it harder to get work.

> **Examiner's comment**
> Two correct factors here. You could also say 'discrimination' or 'previous experience', for example.

(c) One big change in work patterns is that there are many more women working than 25 years ago.

A second change is that there are a lot more part-time jobs today.

More people are now working from home or 'on the move' using new technology ('teleworking').

> **Examiner's comment**
> Three changes in working patterns correctly suggested. Another is weekend working (e.g. the result of more Sunday opening in retail shops).

(d) One way that unemployment statistics may mislead is because of changing definitions – these can artificially change the total. For example, if the definition is changed, it becomes misleading to say there has been a fall in unemployment rate when really it just means fewer people who are out of work get counted as unemployed, just because they don't fit the new definition.

A second way they can be misleading is that not everyone in them is actually unemployed. This then gives a false picture of total unemployment – an overestimate. For example, people who do voluntary (unpaid) work might be registered unemployed but they are actually working, and so are those who work illegally while signing on.

> **Examiner's comment**
> Two ways correctly identified – changing definitions of unemployment and the fact that not everyone 'officially' unemployed is actually unemployed. Both ways clearly explained and discussed, including illustrations.

(e) Sociologists have identified many different social factors influencing leisure. Parker linked leisure to work. He argued that occupation determines leisure pattern. Those in jobs like musicians have an extension pattern – their leisure is a continuation of work, playing music in their spare time. People in routine jobs (e.g. clerical workers) have a neutrality pattern, whereas those in heavy manual jobs have an opposition pattern, spending their leisure recovering. However, pluralists like Roberts argue that other factors like family life cycle also affect leisure patterns, as does whether couples have joint or segregated conjugal roles. Similarly, Gans showed how groups/classes with different educational levels had different leisure tastes (e.g. different music). Age and subculture also affect leisure – punk rockers have different leisure from their parents.

However, according to Item A, 'Roberts claims that work has relatively little influence on people's leisure pursuits'. For example, the unemployed and full-time housewives don't have paid work, so their leisure can't be influenced by work. However, as feminists like Deem argue, women's unpaid work affects their leisure. In a patriarchal society, women's leisure is controlled by their gender role and their subordination to men. For example, they don't have as much time (women in paid work have a double shift of housework as well), and men dominate leisure spaces (e.g. women often can't go in pubs alone, because these are seen as men's spaces). In a male-dominated society, men dominate leisure.

Marxists like Clarke and Critcher argue that capitalism shapes leisure. Capitalism has commercialised leisure, for example football (replica shirts, pay TV and shareholders), the music industry, etc. are all ways of making profits. They also see leisure as shaped by the state, for example in the nineteenth century the state began to regulate leisure (e.g. pubs and music halls had to be licensed by magistrates) as a way of controlling the working class outside work hours.

Postmodernists see leisure as not really 'controlled' by other factors like work, but as something that people freely choose. They see leisure as the main way that people now construct their identities. Instead of being tied to work/production, leisure is about consumption. Fashion, music, sport, holidays, etc. are ways we can create our own identities through our leisure. But leisure is still not a totally free choice (as Roberts in Item A shows), social factors still influence it. For example, the unemployed can't choose to go to festivals or top football matches, which can easily cost as much as someone on benefits gets to live off for a week.

> **Examiner's comment**
> This is a **wide-ranging** answer covering the influence of lots of social factors. Not all of these are covered in detail, but this is OK – you wouldn't be able to do this in the time allowed. But several of them are done quite fully: **work** (a good idea, since the question specifically refers to work), plus gender roles, capitalism and the state, and identity. On top of this, several other influences are identified more briefly – family life cycle, conjugal roles, education, age and subculture. There is also relevant **evaluation** of Roberts and of postmodernism. It lacks a conclusion to round it off, but it's a very strong answer.

(f) Alienation is an important concept in the sociology of work and sociologists disagree about its nature or definition and what causes it. The first major view of alienation was Marx's. He argued that it was separation from one's true self, which we create through our labour, and he saw capitalism as the cause. Capitalism separates workers from the means of production and the product of their labour (these are the property of the capitalists), from other workers and from their true selves. For Marx, alienation would not be overcome until capitalism was overthrown.

Others disagree about the nature and causes of alienation, whether it's inevitable or even exists. Blauner argues that it has four dimensions: powerlessness, meaninglessness, isolation and self-estrangement. The level of alienation depends on the type of technology used, rather than on capitalism. As Item B shows, historically alienation rose with changes in technology, e.g. from craft (low alienation) to its highest in assembly-line production, where workers are powerless (have to work at the speed of the line), isolated (can't move around the work area), work is meaningless because it's fragmented into many small jobs, etc.

However, with automated technology, the trend is reversed – as in Blauner's 'inverted U-curve' (Item B). Unlike Marx, therefore, he believes alienation can be overcome without overthrowing capitalism, but by changing the technology instead. Marxists disagree, arguing that it's still exploitation and the capitalists retain ownership and control.

Goldthorpe and Lockwood's 'action' approach rejects Blauner's positivist search for external causes of alienation. They argue it isn't technology, but workers' orientations to work that count. They found the assembly-line workers in their study were not alienated despite boring jobs, since they didn't work for intrinsic satisfaction but had 'instrumental' motives (money). So long as they earned high wages for their privatised family life styles, they were not dissatisfied. Many had actually given up skilled jobs to take routine jobs for higher wages.

Other writers have tried to combine approaches, i.e. both technology and workers' meanings and expectations of work. But even this is too limited, since we have to look at wider factors like the political traditions and culture of the society. Gallie showed that these were important by comparing the same industry (oil refining) in two different countries, France and the UK, and found that French workers were more 'alienated'.

More recently, postmodernists have argued that Marx's idea of alienation as separation from our true selves is no longer relevant, because we no longer have a single self. In postmodern society, we have multiple or fragmented identities – there is no single self which is the 'true' one, we pick and mix our identities from many different sources, especially the media and leisure.

Examiner's comment

A very well-developed answer, showing a sound knowledge and understanding of a good range of relevant material on alienation. In each case, **relevant concepts** are identified and used correctly, e.g. on Blauner: four dimensions, the role of technology, the inverted U-curve. The answer **uses the Item** (as the question requires), and **different views** are not only described in detail, but are also **evaluated** – e.g. Blauner is criticised by Marxists and Goldthorpe and Lockwood, Marx is criticised by postmodernists, etc.

How to score full marks

(a) A pilot study is a small trial or 'test' study carried out before the main study. It is used to iron out any problems in it, such as respondents not being able to understand questions. These can then be amended before the main questionnaire is sent out.

> **Examiner's comment**
> A clear and very full explanation.

(b) One difference is that in a structured interview, it is common to have closed-ended questions (i.e. ones where the interviewee has to choose an answer from a list given by the interviewer), whereas in an unstructured interview, open-ended questions are more likely to be used and the interviewee is free to answer as they wish.

A second difference is that, in theory, all structured interviews are carried out in the same way (they are standardised), with the same questions, wording, order, tone of voice etc. Unstructured interviews are not standardised, and each one may be unique. This is because different questions, wordings etc. can be used by the interviewer as and when they feel it relevant to do so.

> **Examiner's comment**
> Two relevant differences, very thoroughly explained.

(c) One advantage is that they can cover large numbers of people, giving more representative findings.

Secondly, from a positivist viewpoint, it is an advantage that they can produce quantitative data.

Thirdly, they are not time-consuming – data can be gathered more quickly than by using other primary methods such as interviews or PO.

> **Examiner's comment**
> Three suitable reasons for using questionnaires.

(d) One problem that Festinger and his colleagues might have faced was the problem of 'getting in'. Using their method of covert participant observation means that the researcher has to pretend to be one of the group they are studying, concealing their true identity. This is not always easy; for example, secretive or deviant groups (such as Mrs Keech's group might be) may be suspicious of outsiders seeking membership. For instance, they may impose tests that researchers would be unable or unwilling to take, or require them to adopt a totally new way of life (e.g. renouncing their family).

A second problem is 'getting out'. Once accepted and trusted by members of the group, researchers have moral obligations to them. (They may even 'go native', i.e. become real members of the group rather than just researchers pretending.) They will therefore have to behave unethically in quitting the group – either just 'walking away' without explanation, or they will have to lie about their reasons for going.

> **Examiner's comment**
> Two well-explained problems. Another one would be the danger of one's cover being blown – deviant groups in particular may turn very nasty if they discover you are spying on them. A further problem is that of making notes when studying covertly. (One way Festinger and his colleagues got round this was to take turns going to the toilet, where the researcher would then note down everything that had happened since the previous researcher had been to the toilet!)

(e) Questionnaires are cheap, quick and useful for gathering factual information. However, questionnaires are a less sensitive method than participant observation and unstructured interviews. Firstly, as Item B points out, we are not present when respondents complete the questionnaire, so we don't know whether they have misinterpreted the question and given an invalid answer. For example, Schofield's study of sexual behaviour among young people originally tried to use questionnaires but found respondents didn't always understand the questions. (One young girl's answer to the question 'Are you a virgin?' was 'No, not yet'!) Also, because the respondent is absent when the researcher interprets the answer, misunderstanding can arise here too.

By contrast, an interviewer's presence allows them to clear up any misunderstandings about the meaning of questions and answers. This is why Schofield eventually chose to use interviews instead. An unstructured interview is a more sensitive lie-detector, since the interviewer's presence provides extra evidence (e.g. body language, tone of voice). We can be sure that the right person is answering our questions – whereas questionnaires could be filled out by someone else.

Likewise, participant observation is more effective because we can see for ourselves what people really do rather than just rely on written answers, where they may lie, exaggerate or forget. As Whyte noted, you can learn more by sitting and watching than by asking questions – including questionnaires. This is especially true with 'delicate' topics such as deviance, religious beliefs etc. Sociologists have used covert PO to study topics like homosexuality in public toilets (Humphreys), fiddling among bread roundsmen (Ditton) and, as in Item A, religions who predict the end of the world is nigh (Festinger). With deviant groups, a stranger giving out questionnaires would be met with suspicion and refusal. Groups who cannot read or write, like non-literate societies, cannot be studied using written questionnaires. Participant observation is a good alternative method in these circumstances, putting the researcher in a position to see for themselves how the group lives. This is the method of 'verstehen' or empathy (Weber), where you put yourself in the shoes of the subject and see the world as they see it.

Feminists argue that positivist methods like questionnaires reflect false patriarchal assumptions about women's experiences. Hilary Graham argues that oppressed groups cannot always put a name to the things that oppress them, so the questionnaire is of no use. A more sensitive and equal relationship between female subjects and researchers is important to get at the reality of women's lives, such as an unstructured interview or conversation between equals which allows the oppressed to find a voice. Oakley's study 'From Here to Maternity' makes extensive use of this method.

PO and unstructured interviews are interpretivist methods. They allow people to speak for themselves and provide rich, valid, qualitative data sensitive to their feelings and meanings, whereas questionnaires with closed-ended questions are less sensitive. As Hughes argues, because questionnaires only allow the respondent to choose from a list of pre-selected answers, they merely impose the researcher's meanings.

> **Examiner's comment**
> This is a good answer. First, it keeps firmly **focused** on the question of the advantages of PO and unstructured interviews over questionnaires. It doesn't drift off into a general answer listing the many advantages and disadvantages of the three methods – which is just as well because it would take hours to list all of them! Second – as the question requires – it deals with **both** PO and unstructured interviews and how each of them is more useful than questionnaires. It shows awareness of **different approaches** – for example, interpretive, feminist and positivist – and finally, it makes very good use of a range of **studies** which have used the different methods.

(f) It is true that practical issues are important when it comes to choosing research methods. However, theoretical perspective and ethics are both important factors.

Two obvious practical issues are time and money. Some methods are cheaper than others. As Item B notes, more people can be surveyed by postal questionnaire than by face-to-face interviews for the same money. Source of funding may also dictate certain methods, e.g. official sources often prefer quantitative results since these are seen as more scientific. This would favour questionnaires or structured interviews.

Similarly, questionnaires are quick to administer (though they take time to draw up and pilot), whereas PO can take years (e.g. Whyte took four years). For example, it can take a long time to get accepted by a group and also the researcher is dependent on events and other people, whereas in an interview, the interviewer dictates the situation.

Another practical factor is the nature of the group or topic, together with the researcher's personal skills and characteristics. For example, Dobash and Dobash studied domestic violence using interviews. It would be hard to use PO, since you would not easily gain access to the homes of wife batterers – although you might use PO in a women's refuge. Similarly, your age, gender, ethnicity/race, class, accent etc. might all affect whether you could do covert (or even overt) PO. Downes and Rock note that not everybody can 'pass' as a Hell's Angel or punk rocker! However, the white sociologist Griffin used drugs to change his skin pigment to black so he could observe racial discrimination first hand.

Apart from practical matters, however, there is also the researcher's theoretical perspective. Generally, Marxists and functionalists, who take a 'macro', structural view, favour quantitative methods such as questionnaires and structured interviews. These can be used to test hypotheses and establish laws. By contrast, interactionists take a 'micro' view, seeking qualitative data which gives them empathy and a 'feel' for people's meanings, so they prefer PO or unstructured interviews. But sometimes this is overridden by practical issues. For example, the functionalist Malinowski studied the Trobriand Islanders by using PO, since this was the best way to grasp how a strange culture works. For instance, the Islanders were illiterate, so written questionnaires would have been no use.

Finally, many argue that it is wrong to research people without their informed consent. This can be an issue especially with covert PO, where the researcher deliberately deceives the group about his/her identity and aims. Some experiments, such as those by Milgram who misled subjects into thinking they were inflicting electric shocks on people, have also been criticised as unethical. Thus, while practical issues are important, ethical and theoretical issues must also be taken into consideration when choosing a research method.

Examiner's comment
This answer has a good, **clear structure** which allows the examiner to see where it is going. The student shows a good knowledge and understanding of a range of sociological material on practical, theoretical and ethical issues in research. Several **practical** factors, such as time, money, the source of funding, the topic and group being studied and the personal skills and characteristics of the researcher, can all play a part in affecting the choice of method. The answer then goes on to consider two **other** important influences – **theoretical perspective** and **ethics**. Throughout the answer, information from **studies** is used to illustrate the arguments, the points made are **evaluated** and relevant conclusions are drawn from them.